KIDPRENEUR 101
A Build Your Business Guide for Ages 8-18

Copyright © 2016 Danette O'Neal
All rights reserved.
ISBN-13:978-1539061793
ISBN-10:1539061795

About the Author

Dr. Danette O'Neal, Author- MONEY MATTERS 101; LEED educator, HGTV alumna, entrepreneur, and trainer is the Broker/Owner of Danette O'Neal Realtors (DOR) with offices in the Greater New Orleans and Atlanta Metro areas.

Dr. O'Neal specializes in residential and commercial sales, property management and spiritual architecture. With more than 26 years in real estate, she regularly lends her expertise to nonprofit organizations to expand their missions. In 2009 she founded *DOR Referral and Asset Management,* a micro-business firm that specializes in financial fitness course development, entrepreneurial training, and consulting for organizational leadership and sustainability. Her focus is on supporting organizations to grow through engaging their people with executive and business coaching, strategic planning and the facilitation of a range of leadership development programs.

She holds a PhD in Public Policy and Administration, a Masters in Public Administration both from Walden University, and a M.A. in Community Economic Development from Southern New Hampshire University. She is a Professor and SME for Strayer and Realtor University in the Schools of Business, Real Estate, and Public Administration. Dr. O'Neal is serving nationally on State and Local Issues, Professional Development Committees for the National Association of Realtors. She volunteers as an interpreter for the deaf and is a leader in the Full Gospel Baptist Church International Hearing Impaired Ministry.

Foreword

I have known Dr. Danette O'Neal for over 13 years as a highly successful real estate broker, dynamic entrepreneur, brilliant public speaker, progressive educator and wonderful mother. Her foresight in writing *Kidpreneur101* distinguishes her from many promoters of entrepreneurship in that, she wisely focuses on youth. According to the New York Times best seller *The Millionaire Next Door*, authors Stanley and Danko state, "two thirds of all millionaires are self-employed" as America continues to eliminate jobs through advances in technology, entrepreneurship has become even more important.

The minds of children are open free and unencumbered by the barriers that adults have learned over time; therefore, their minds are ripe for the development of habits that could inure to profound entrepreneurial success. Napoleon Hill, in his timeless book, *Think and Grow Rich* stated, "that imagination is the workshop of the mind". Children have incredible imaginations, and Dr. O'Neal recognizes that we should never underestimate the power of a young vibrant mind. In this book, Dr. O'Neal shares with her reader the very terms of entrepreneurial art that every business owner should know. She engages the children reading her book in activities that develop their entrepreneurial thinking and actually encourages the development of businesses. From sharing various corporate structures, the history of money, to explaining cash, checks or credit, she immerses the reader into the world of capitalism.

As a child growing up, I was enamored with the idea of Snowball Stands and thought about opening up stands in different parts of the country. I would have greatly benefitted from *Kidpreneur 101*. As a teenager, I started a business called *Gift Raps*. Gift Raps produced rap jingles as promos for corporate businesses and its owners. In the mid 1980s, this concept was ahead of its time. In subsequent years, this very concept was used to bill multi-million-dollar corporate television commercials. Had I been apprised of the principles in Kidpreneur 101, there is no doubt I could have grown that business into a very lucrative operation.

Today, as the owner of a highly successful civil trial law firm and a real estate development company, I am inspired by the entrepreneurial wisdom embodied in Kidpreneur 101; moreover, as the parent of a 14 year-old budding entrepreneur, this book is mandatory reading for my son.

James Carter, Esq.
Former New Orleans City Councilman
New Orleans Criminal Justice Commissioner
University of Louisiana System Board of Supervisors
VERA Institute of Justice Fellow
2015 Litigator Award

Table of Contents

	About this Book	6
	To the Parents: How to Use This Book	8
Part 1	Teaching Kidpreneur Thinking	9
	Kidpreneur Thinking	10
	Kidpreneur Case Studies & Activity(s)	13
	Kidpreneur Thinking (Discussion)	15
Part 2	How Money Works	16
	What is Money	17
	The History of Paper Money	18
	Banking	20
	Cash, Checks, or Credit	21
	How Do Banks Work	22
	Kidpreneur Activity (Word Scrabble)	24
	Kidpreneur Activity (Bundles of Money)	25
	How to Read the Stock Market Pages (Intro)	26
	Are You Ready for the Real World	28
	Kidpreneur Investing Tips	29
	Stock Market Activity (Assignment)	31
	Your Competitive Strategy	34
Part 3	"_____" the Kidpreneur	35
	Real Ideas for Making Money	37
	Real Life Kidpreneurs (Kidz's Food Truck Business)	39
	Kidnovation	41
	Kidpreneur Interview Form	43
	Kidpreneur Decision Grid	44
	Yikes…Before You Open	45
	For & Against Template	47
Part 4	Kidpreneur Business Plan	48
	5 Questions to Ask Before Starting a Business	49
	Developing Your Business Profile	50
	Company Profile Worksheet	52
	What is Cash Flow?	53
	Cash Flow Statement (Template)	54
	Corporate Structures	55
	Kidpreneur Planning (Business Plan Template)	57
	1-page Business Plan	61
	Check Your Understanding (Activity)	62

Part 5	Business Operations	64
	How Big is Your Slice of the Pie?	65
	How is Your Pie Divided?	66
	Understanding Fixed and Variable Cost	67
	Kidpreneur Activity: Projecting Your Profits	68
	Comparing Gross Revenue & Net Profit	69
	Kidpreneur Comprehension: Projecting Profit/Essay	70
	Kidnovation	72
	Kidpreneur Traits	73
	Determining Demand	74
	Creating Demand	76
	Lisa's Courier Service- Discussion/Activity	77
	How Will You Use Your Money?	78
	Cost Related Terms	79
Part 6	Managing The Business	80
	Workers, Employees & Independent Contractors	81
	Hiring Workers/ Preparing for the Interview	82
Part 7	Financing	84
	Secured & Unsecured Loans	85
	The Balance Sheet	86
	Income Statements & Templates	88
	Credit Reporting	90
	Keeping Good Credit	92
	Meeting With the Banker	93
	Decision Grid (Activity)	94
	Funding Sources	96
	Buying an Existing Business	97
	Evaluating the Purchase of and Existing Business	98
	Pros & Cons Decision Grid	100
	Kidpreneur Forrest Mars (Discussion Questions)	101
	Kidpreneur Milton Hershey (Discussion Questions)	103
	Taxes & Insurance	106
	Final Thoughts	107
Reading List		108
Appendix		109
Glossary	Build Your Own Glossary (Activity)	110
	Acknowledgements	115

About this Book

TEACHING KIDPRENUER THINKING

I had my first job *real job* at age 12. I worked for a company similar to Avon and had checks amounting to more than $800 before I told my Mom about my business venture (in 1973 this was a small fortune). You see at age 12, I was still too young to open a checking account and I needed to cash my checks. I had survived off of the cash sales for six months. That's how I reordered the cosmetic products and fulfilled my customer's orders. But now it was time to buy the guitar I wanted and I needed to cash in.

The very next year at age 13, I realized that a hobby had developed into quite a skill set. I not only sold and design all of my clothes in high school but earned money doing it for others. I began designing ball gowns, making costumes for children and carnival organizations, choir robes, bed linens, and just about anything that anyone hired me to do. The business was really good and it continued well into my adult years.

Along the way, I opened a children's clothing store The Kidds Closet, ran our family owned Daycare center, and leased a movie theater all before age 25. As a young woman, I understood how money worked. This led at age 28 to obtaining my insurance, securities and real estate licenses and embarking on what has now been a life long journey of teaching others how to become financially independent through entrepreneurism.

If you are already a *Kidpreneur,* I know that you are enthusiastic, tenacious, have commonsense, are determined and want some financial independence. Most of us are born with at least two out of the four traits. A college education, later will push you further and validate some of your decision-making. What you don't possess now can be learned through mentorship, watching others, and reading. Thus, the purpose of this book!

Kidprerner-thinking involves you learning organizational skills that will build your business and help you operate more efficiently. **Kidpreneurs invent things as a tool to effect change, to do some type of good, or to fill a void in society.** This will lead to healthy households, stronger communities, and stronger local economies. A good economy means that there are enough jobs for people to afford food, homes and necessities. If you understand how money works and how money grows, then you'll be ready to draft your business and marketing plan. All of this is important to reducing risk and increasing profits, of course! This is what adults call financial literacy.

Why begin your *Kidpreneur* journey learning by trial and error when there's a written guide here to help you. *Kidpreneur 101* begins at the basics, teaching you the basics of business planning. We explore the four major financial sectors: banking, real estate, insurance, and the stock market, the types of business organizations, managing employees, marketing and taxes. There are tons of worksheets to help you get your business started and to guide you all along the way. Have some fun with this book and if you like it *buy* another for a friend.

Dr. Danette O'Neal

YOU CAN DO ANYTHING, BUT YOU CAN'T DO EVERYTHING.

To the Parent: How to Use This Book

HOW TO RAISE A KIDPRENEUR:

Teaching children about business and money at a very young age is important for the future of our economy as a whole. So what does it take to raise a Kidpreneur? Why cultivate a Kidpreneur mindset in your child? The main reason is because, they will need it more than the previous generations did! The world of work is changing rapidly. It is estimated that within the next 5 to 10 years more than 45% of the United States workforce will be freelancers, contractors, part-timers, and self-employed individuals.

Research shows that children of successful business people gain and an important financial advantage and informal training in entrepreneurship; however, if the parent is not an entrepreneur, you can still get your most precious asset to start thinking about ideas and values that they can later carry into their professional adult lives.

Kidpreneur 101 defines and teaches ages 8 to 18 entrepreneurship, brainstorming, goal setting, how money is multiplied, business planning, and resilience through investing and using the stock market to build their business.

This book is filled with real life stories, worksheets, activities, and special assignments to promote leadership, Kidpreneur thinking, and *Kidnovation*. Regardless of what your child grows up to do, they will need an entrepreneurial skill set to do it well. Kidpreneur 101 validates the need for the strategic management of entrepreneurship education.

Part 1
TEACHING KIDPRENUER THINKING

Objectives:
- Kidpreneurs (Ages 8-18) will be able to identify entrepreneurship opportunities by personal distinguishing characteristics.
- Kidpreneurs will be able to define entrepreneurship, identify the characteristics within themselves, and understand which ones they are lacking or need to develop.

Discussions:
- What is entrepreneurship?
- The 4 types of entrepreneurs?
- What is a Kidpreneur?
- What are the characteristics of a Kidpreneur?
- How do you know that you are a Kidpreneur?

BASIC VOCABULARY:
advertising
business
cost
consumers
capitol
entrepreneur
goods
Kidnovators
liability
loss
labor
price
production
profit
risk
services

Kidpreneur Thinking

What do you want to be when you grow up? Some of you may have ambitions to be a scientist, doctor, teacher, or lawyer; others may want to open their own business. Still many of you will want to do both. You will need to learn the definitions of the following terms:

1. **Business-** The selling of goods or services for the sake of earning a profit.
2. **Entrepreneur-** A person who starts a business and assumes the risk for the purpose of making a profit.
3. **Goods-** Tangible (something you can feel/touch) items that can be bought or sold.
4. **Services-** Intangible, an economic activity, labor for a fee, a valuable action to fulfill a need or demand.

What is a **Kidpreneur**?
A Kidpreneur is someone who takes the initiative to design, organize, or invent a new business venture, or create an opportunity for economic growth. He or she is a decision-maker who decides how, and how much a service can be sold for or produced.

A *Kidpreneur* is a risk taker who controls the business opportunity (**capital and labor**). **Goods** are things that people can use and enjoy. These can include toys, electronics, shoes, school supplies, or cars. **Services** are actions that satisfy consumer wants. These may include changing the oil in an automobile, a plumber repairing a broken pipe, the barber, or the guy who cuts your parents lawn.

The word Kidpreneur is adapted from the French 1723 root word entrepreneur. The term *entrepreneur* was first used by the Irish Economist Richard Cantillon. He said an entrepreneur is "one who undertakes an enterprise, and acts as a connector between capital *(money)* and labor".
http://en.wikipedia.org/wiki/Entrepreneur

Being a Kidpreneur (entrepreneur) is not always the same as running a business; though, we will learn in the upcoming chapters that the two may overlap significantly. Kidpreneurs satisfy consumers wants. Consumers are shoppers.

Kidpreneurs are:
- *Kidnovators* are comfortable in leadership roles,
- Are independent and self reliant,
- Optimistic and strive for excellence,
- Team builders,
- Creative and have the willingness to learn and develop personally, and
- Hard-working and willing to take risks.

Richard Branson gives six tips for Kidpreneurs who want to start their own businesses, of course I added about 114 pages to it:

Number one, think about what drives you. What talents do you already have? What are some of the things that you are passionate about? What are some of the things that you already can do *really really* well?

Remember we discussed this in **Money Matters 101 page 25**. By the way, if you do not have a copy, take a pause here, grab the book, and read it first. It will help you be a better Kidpreneur.

Are you good at gardening? Can you speak a second language? Have you already developed great cooking skills? Can you sew, crochet or knit? Are you good at computers, have you learned how to code or make an app? Can you fulfill a market need? Is there something unique about the service you can provide? If you already have a business in mind, or a product that you feel you will be good at marketing, will it improve other people's lives?

Next, ask your parents for some smart advice. If your parents are not entrepreneur's, ask another family member, your teacher, or someone else that has been in the same business or something similar to yours. Go to the Internet and read everything you can and don't let anyone tell you that you're not going to be a success!

Make sure you write all of your dreams and your goals down on paper. This will keep you focused and motivated while you are on your journey. Set weekly goals and targets. Make long-term plans for the quarter and year. Celebrate yourself at each milestone.

Last, you *gotta* love what you do! *Kidpreneurship* should be fun. I have met a lot of unhappy-wealthy people in business. There is a lot of work involved in being your own boss. It can be frustrating; but, at the end of the day, you should have no regrets. I'm reminded about a song Frank Sinatra recorded in 1969 long before many of you or some of your parents were born, " I did it my way". Google it!

Kidpreneur Thinking
(4 Main types of Kidpreneurs)

shaping entrepreneurs of all kinds!

1. The first and not ranked in order of significance is the *Business Kidpreneur* (BK)- he's/she's the idea generator, the CEO, the force driving the company. Example: Oprah Winfrey: http://www.forbes.com/profile/oprah-winfrey/

2. The second is the *Trade Kidpreneur* (TK)- she's/he's the manufacturer and is good at brand building. The TK has built a product and focuses on brand. (Example: Henry Ford, Dave Thomas the founder of Wendy's – read Dave's story and listen to the video at: http://www.biography.com/people/dave-thomas-9542110)

3. The third is the *Kidnovator* (KN). He's/she's the developer, the engineer, or the tech person. (Example Steve Jobs: http://allaboutstevejobs.com/bio/shortbio.php)

4. The last one is the *Social Kidpreneur* (SK)- he's/she's the person who creates jobs for others. The SK is fueled by passion and motivation. These individuals use their talent to develop business ventures that address social, cultural, or environmental issues. (Chelsea Clinton- https://en.wikipedia.org/wiki/Chelsea_Clinton)

KIDPRENEUR Activity

After reading Dave Thomas's story, the founder of Wendy's:
http://www.biography.com/people/dave-thomas-9542110

1. Where did Dave Thomas work when he got the vision to open his own restaurant?

2. Who or what influenced Dave Thomas to open his own restaurant?

3. What was the risk for Dave Thomas?

4. How did Dave make Wendy's different from other hamburger restaurants?

5. What entrepreneur characteristics did Dave Thomas have?

6. Did /Does Dave Thomas or Wendy's give back to the community?

7. Did you know about Dave Thomas before reading the story in Kidpreneur101?

KIDPRENEUR Activity:

Read or listen to the short story of Australian Kidpreneur- Mikaila Ulmer of Bee Sweet Lemonade (*Me & Bee's Lemonade)*. Her handmade product is on the shelves of retailers in several states, including Whole Foods. She recently appeared on Shark Tank' and cut a huge deal to expand her company.

Read her story at:
http://meandthebees.com/pages/about-us, visit her Facebook page at: https://www.facebook.com/MikailasBees/ or the YouTube video's:
https://www.youtube.com/watch?v=Q1VVzmXrmwg
https://www.youtube.com/watch?v=xYwTAJMbFy8

1. How old was Mikailia when she first became a Kidpreneur?

2. Who or what influenced Mikailia to open her own restaurant?

3. What special Kidpreneur characteristics did Mikailia have?

4. What was the risk for *Mikaila & **Me & Bee's Lemonade?***

5. Did you know about *Mikaila & **Me & Bee's Lemonade*** before reading it here in Kidpreneur 101?

KIDPRENEUR Thinking

Are you, or do you want to be a Kidpreneur?

Name one reward a Kidpreneur will enjoy in starting a business?

What major characteristics do you think Kidpreneurs need to process?

What economic concepts did you learn in Part 1?

Part 2
How Money Works?

OBJECTIVES

Kidpreneurs, will begin using the terms Kidpreneurship, and Kidnovation interchangeably, and apply the terms to real life local and national businessmen, women and children who are carving a market niche.

- Kidpreneurs will be able to use this knowledge to explain how how different and difficult the world would be without money.
- Kidpreneurs will improve counting skills, develop counting skills, and gain skills determining the dollar dimensions that make up certain sums.
- Kidpreneurs will understand that money makes it easier to trade, borrow, save, invest and compare the value of goods and services.

BASIC VOCABULARY:
Banking
Bartering
Bureau of Engraving and Printing
Credit Unions
Stock Market
M1
Shareholder
Treasury Notes

"It is said that Money makes the world go around. It's true! This chapter, "How Money Works" is perhaps the largest and most important chapter in this book. Kidpreneurship education begins with fundamentally understanding real life opportunities and real world risk".

Dr. D. O'Neal

What is Money?

We all know how to use money, right? But do you understand where it came from? Before dollar bills were created, or coins formed from gold, there was a barter system. Basically, two individuals each possessed something of value that the other wanted or needed. They would trade and enter an informal agreement to meet basic needs.

This early form of bartering proved to be exhausting, and inefficient. People looked for a more efficient means for paying for goods and services. Did you know that tobacco was once used for money? Some of the first money or currency used by Colonialist was beaver pelts and dried corn. Beaver pelts and dried corn was considered valuable, durable, portable, and easily stored. These were all used to barter. If a baker needed grain to bake, and a fisherman needed bread- they would trade the fish for the loaf of bread, and the baker, of course would strike up a deal with tobacco farmer who also supplied the grain.

Then came gold. Foreign governments were able to take their U.S. currency and exchange it for gold with the U.S. Like the beaver pelts and dried corn, gold was and still is valuable. Gold has always been desirable. Many people in the Wild-Wild West have been killed for it, Pharaohs have been buried with it, and the army even built a special non-penetrable place to store it for the government – Fort Knox.

Where is Money Printed

The Bureau of Engraving and Printing has been pressing all the United States' currency since 1877. It's hard to believe, but this process began as a six-person team operating in the basement of the Department of Treasury. We've come a long way. Today's operation employs over 2,300 employees that occupy twenty-five acres of floor space in two Washington, D.C. buildings. The United States Treasury also maintains a satellite printing plant in Ft. Worth, Texas. Currency (bills) are engraved, and printed twenty-four hours a day on 30 high speed presses. Over $200 million in notes are printed each 24 hours. Wow!

- *http://www.historyworld.net/wrldhis/PlainTextHistories.asp?historyid=ab14*
- http://www.businessinsider.com/the-history-of-the-100000-bill-2013-1
- http://www.wsj.com/articles/SB10001424052748703709804575202270657107814

History of Paper Money

1690 - The Massachusetts Bay Colony issued the first paper money in the colonies that would later form the United States.

1775 - American colonists issued paper currency for the Continental Congress to finance the Revolutionary War. The notes were backed by the "anticipation" of tax revenues. Without solid backing and easily counterfeited, the notes quickly became devalued, giving rise to the phrase "not worth a continental".

1781 - To support the Revolutionary War, the Continental Congress chartered the Bank of North America in Philadelphia as the nation's first "real" bank.

1791 - After adoption of the Constitution in 1789, Congress chartered the first Bank of the United States until 1811 and authorized it to issue paper bank notes to eliminate confusion and simplify trade. The bank served as the U.S. Treasury's fiscal agent, thus performing the first central bank functions.

1861 - On the brink of bankruptcy and pressed to finance the Civil War, Congress authorized the United States Treasury to issue paper money for the first time in the form of non-interest bearing Treasury Notes call Demand Notes.

1865 - Gold Certificates were issued by the Department of the Treasury against gold coin and bullion deposits and were circulated until 1933.

1877 - The Department of the Treasury's Bureau of Engraving and Printing started printing all U.S. currency.

1913 - After the financial panics of 1893 and 1907, the Federal Reserve Act of 1913 was passed. It created the Federal Reserve System as the nation's central bank to regulate the flow of money and credit for economic stability and growth. The system was authorized to issue Federal Reserve Notes, now the only U.S. currency produced.

1929 - Currency was reduced in size by twenty-five percent and standardized with uniform portraits on the faces and emblems and monuments on the backs.

1990 - A security thread and micro printing were introduced in $50 and $100 notes to deter counterfeiting by technologically advanced copiers and printers.

1996 - Additional security features are added to a newly redesigned $100 Federal Reserve note. The note incorporates both familiar and new features, while remaining recognizably American. Redesigned lower denominations are being introduced at the rate of about one denomination per year.

1997 - The new $50 bill is introduced. The reverse side includes an enlarged number 50 in the lower right-hand corner to aid the low-vision community.

2016- Harriett Tubman (former slave and abolitionist) will replace Andrew Jackson on the $20 bill. While Hamilton would remain on the $10, and Abraham Lincoln on the $5, images of women would be added to the back of both. Tubman would be the first woman honored on paper currency since Martha Washington's portrait briefly graced the $1 silver certificate in the late 19th century (http://www.nytimes.com/2016/04/21/us/women-currency-treasury-harriet-tubman.html?_r=0).

The picture of the Treasury building on the back of the $10 bill would be replaced with a picture of the 1913 march in support of women's right to vote that ended at the building, along with portraits of five suffrage leaders: Lucretia Mott, Sojourner Truth, Elizabeth Cady Stanton, Alice Paul and Susan B. Anthony, who in more recent years was on an unpopular $1 coin until minting ceased.

On the flip side of the $5 bill, the Lincoln Memorial would remain, but an image of Marian Anderson's 1939 performance at the Memorial along with images of Eleanor Roosevelt, who arranged Anderson's Lincoln Memorial performance, and the Rev. Dr. Martin Luther King Jr., who in 1963 delivered his "I have a dream" speech from its steps will be added. This is all slated for unveiling in 2020.

Sources:
http://www.moneyfactory.gov/uscurrency/2note.html
http://www.investopedia.com/articles/basics/03/061303.asp.
http://currency-history.info/history-of-american-currency

Banking

A bank or credit union is a place where people can save or store their money. It's more efficient than your piggy bank at home, and much safer. By the way, now that you are on your way to making big money, no piggy bank will be able to hold it. The bank will pay you (interest) if you keep your money there. The more money you put in the bank, the more they will pay you.

Many adults use banks and credit unions to help them manage their money. Money is a form of an exchange and it is widely used because bartering (trading) is just not as efficient as it used to be. In order for money to be call currency it must have four characteristics:
1. It must be generally excepted,
2. Durable,
3. easy to carry, and
4. easily divided.

M1 is what we call the money supply. It's a tally of all the coins, paper money and the balances of everybody's checking account in all the banks in the entire world. Wow!

Want to know more bout banking? **Banking on our future:** http://bit.ly/2ctalid is an interactive drag & drop program on the web that will teach you more about banking. Students can register for free. You will have to answer some questions about your age, gender, and how you heard about the site. Have some fun with it.

Note: Credit cards are not considered money, because they are not accepted everywhere, and you incur debt when you use them.

"CASH, CHECKS OR CREDIT"
Do you know these financial terms?

1. Bank account for savings.
2. Money is sometimes called _____.
3. Annual Percentage Rate.
4. To sign on the back of a check.
5. A checking account and a savings account are examples of a (2 words)
6. Certificate of Deposit.
7. A drive up bank machine
8. 100 cents.
9. Small box used to store valuables.
10. To take money out of a bank account.
11. To put money into a bank account
12. A charge/penalty for use of a credit card.
13. 25 cents.
14. The maximum amount of money you can borrow.
15. An entire book of forms for writing checks.
16. Checks must be written in _____ (not lead).
17. When you write checks and there is not enough money in your account. You are said to be _____.
18. Legal document used when buying a home.
19. Written promise to a bank to pay money.
20. Metal, gold money
21. 1 cent.
22. Bank reports of your account.
23. Where gold is kept.
24. 5 cents.
25. A Plastic card used to pay for merchandise.
26. Fee for spending more money than is in your checking account is called a _____ charge.
27. 10 cents
28. A person who is out of money and cannot pay their debts is said to be _____.
29. Signing the back of a check:
30. A bank account for paying bills, or writing checks

Write Your Answers Here:

1 _____	16 _____
2 _____	17 _____
3 _____	18 _____
4 _____	19 _____
5 _____	20 _____
6 _____	21 _____
7 _____	22 _____
8 _____	23 _____
9 _____	24 _____
10 _____	25 _____
11 _____	26 _____
12 _____	27 _____
13 _____	28 _____
14 _____	29 _____
15 _____	30 _____

How Do Banks Work

Monies brought to the bank or credit unions for safe-keeping are called **deposits**. One of the best things about saving, is the money they pay you for (interest) using your money. Surprised? It may be a bit confusing, but, banks use your money to lend money to other people. That's right! Kidpreneurs like yourself go to the bank to borrow money to start or expand their businesses, and the bank loans them some of your money! The borrower pays interest. The bank takes a portion, and gives you a portion. This occurs overnight (almost every night) while you're sleeping. The longer you keep your money in the bank the more interest you earn.

Some Tips on Saving

Saving is easy for some Kidpreneurs, but for others it takes a real big effort. That means resisting the urge to go shopping or buying a new piece of equipment for your business.

Here are some tips on how you can get started:

1. First set a goal, then decide on amount that you can *deposit* every single week from of your profits. I'm often asked how much should I be saving? Well, see if you can start with 10% of your income. If you cannot start with 10% then reduce it to 5% or 3% of your income (your net income). Get a notebook and begin writing down all the money that you spend *(see the Money Matters 101 section on Spending Diaries).* If you can see where your money is going, you will probably be more successful in reaching your saving goals.

2. You will need to cut your expenses. So, that means that the $4.53 cup of cappuccino every morning is out! Look for a coupon, or wait for a sale during the holidays and buy a machine to make your own at home.

3. You need to be a smart shopper. There will be a constant need or desire for equipment or supplies as you develop new ways to expand your business. Become an expert researcher. Try online shopping, or buying supplies outside of the immediate vicinity of your business.

4. Last, stay focused! You need to safeguard your money. That's why saving is so important. Kidpreneurs must always be prepared for trouble. This can range from supplies not arriving on time, a dissatisfied customer, hiring extra help during the holidays, extended snow days, hurricanes, or floods that could delay the delivery of products and services. Adults deal with these same things everyday. Kidpreneurs are no different.

These habits will carry you into adulthood and help you take advantage of opportunities to expand when they come along. Mastering ways to stash cash is safeguarding *you* personally and professionally

KIDPRENEUR Activity:
Word Scrabble

1. Folks who work at the Western Currency Facility, the President of the United States, and a National Park ranger, are all people who work for the Federal [vnegetnomr] _____.

2. A [aels] _____ is the name of a sea mammal and also the word for a symbol on the face of a dollar note.

3. Currency is printed using a machine called a [gritsinpserpn] _____ _____.

4. If cows had a word for money, it might be [ahmolo] _____.

5. The Western Currency Facility is part of the [ueruab] _____ of Engraving and Printing.

6. Whether it's paper or coins, it's all [oeynm] _____.

7. $100,000 is the highest [onmntaediion] _____ note that the Bureau of Engraving and Printing has ever produced.

8. The security features included in $20 notes beginning in 2003 make them more difficult to [otniuecrfte] _____.

9. The name of the Bureau of Engraving and Printing facility in Fort Worth, Texas is then Western [errcucny] _____ Facility.

10. [gakecebrn] _____ is a slang term for American currency. It came about because of the color on the back of the notes.

11. Benjamin [nrnakifl] _____ was one of the authors of the Declaration of Independence. He's also on the $100 dollar note.

12. The Bureau of Engraving and Printing is part of the U.S. [eyutsarr]_____ Department.

13. $1, $5, $10, and $20 are all denominations of currency or [eotns] _____.

14. When you put money into a savings or checking account, it's called, "making a _____. [tdsiope]

KIDPRENEUR Activity

Bundles of Money

In the empty spaces write the *value numbers* using words. Look at the example below. Keep in mind the commas separate the place value groups, for example: $XXX,XXX,XXX,XXX.

billions			millions			thousands			hundred			cents	
5	4	6	8	8	8	9	8	8	7	5	4	2	0

$546,888,988,754.20

Now write out the following numbers using words.
For example, $297,143 = two hundred ninety-seven thousand, one hundred forty-three dollars.

1. $5648 =
_____

2. $987,748.00 =
_____

3. $202,283,334.00=
_____

1. Mom bought a new washer and dryer for five hundred twenty dollars on sale. Write this number _____.
2. Nine hundred sixty-four thousand, five hundred, twenty-two = _ _ _ , _ _ _.

3. Four hundred seventy-two million, one hundred eighty-five thousand, eight hundred ninety-seven _ _ _ , _ _ _ , _ _
4. Three hundred forty-seven billion, six hundred sixty-six million, two hundred forty-four thousand, six hundred fifty-one = _ _ _ , _ _ _ , _ _ _ , _ _ _

5. Allen recycles cans. Last month he cashed-in and earned forty-six dollars and twenty –eight cents. How would you write the number? _____.

6. Last year the LA County school district voted to spend 2.6 million dollars to put computer labs in 15 schools. How would you write this number? _____.

8. Dad surprised Mom with a new Corvette on Mother's Day. He spent a whopping fifty-two thousand, two hundred and ninety dollars? Write the number _____ _____.

How to Read the Stock Pages
Introduction

Have you ever looked at the stock pages in the newspaper and wondered how to read them? Well truthfully, they're not at all that hard to read. In fact, it's quite easy! Just read on and you will understand it soon enough.

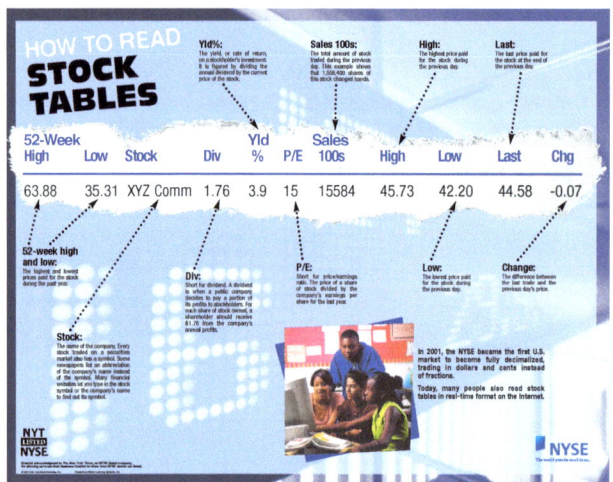

The **stock market** is the place where stocks are bought and sold. Some examples of a stock market that may seem familiar to you is the **New York Stock Exchange** (NYSE), the **American Stock Exchange** (AMEX), the **National Association of Securities Dealers Automated Quotation** (NASDAQ), and the **DOW** (Dow Jones & Company, Inc.).

What are Stocks?
Stocks are pieces of a company. When you own stock from a specific company, you literally own a piece of everything they own. This includes equipment, land, buildings, etc. Let's say you own 100 shares of a company who has sold about 1,000 shares. You now consequently own about 10% of the company. Also, as a stockholder, you have the right to participate in all voting in that specific company. Each share equals 1 vote, and is an indication of how well or bad the company is doing.

Now it's time to learn how to read the actual stocks listed in your local newspaper and on the Internet.

52-Week					Yld		Vol				Net
Hi	Lo	Stock		Div	%	PE	100s	Hi	Lo	Close	Chg
15.36	7.28	Sample	SPL	.56	3.8	22	215	12.34	7.75	12.67	-11.92

Above is an example of what a stock listing looks like. We'll go over what each abbreviation means and what those numbers are. There is a common misconception that you must be a certain age, say 18 or older, to be able to own, purchase, or sell stocks. This statement is 100% false. There is no age limitation placed on selling or purchasing stocks. You are eligible to purchase and sell shares of any stock at any age.

Keep in mind that not all growth rates are the same. If your bank is paying 3% interest on your savings, that's pretty much guaranteed money. If a savings bond is paying you 5% interest, that is pretty close to a sure thing also. (Interest rates change over time, so your bank might be paying you 1% in some years and 6% in others).

The stock market is not a sure thing, and neither are companies that issue bonds. Stock market returns fluctuate. There are good years, great years, so-so years, and years we'd much rather forget. Over long periods of time, though, the stock market tends to go up. Over many decades, it has averaged an annual 11% return.

Similarly, with companies, many remain strong for decades or a century. Others fail. If you select and invest in solid, growing companies, you can hope to earn as much as 15%, on average, per year. If you select one or more companies that turn out to be remarkable growers, such as Microsoft, the average growth rate for your investments might be higher than 15%.

In general, the more certain the growth rate, the lower the risk will be. The more speculative the higher the risk may be. We'll cover these topics in more detail later. For now, just understand that most growth rates are not sure things. *(That's okay, though. You can still make a lot of money by investing).*

Have you heard about ACORN? It's an APP and an easy way for you or your parents to invest your spare change from your daily purchases. Download it, open a small account, and watch how quickly it adds up.

Are you ready for the real world?

So, are you ready for the real world? The stock market can be a great place for a Kidpreneur to raise some big money for expansion. If you need cash, you can sell pieces of your company in the stock market. If the public likes your goods and services, they can buy shares or pieces of your company and turn it into an even bigger enterprise.

By now you understand a little bit about risk and return, but by the time you get to Chapter 4 you will really have a grasp of it. My philosophy is... *no risk no return*. Many businesses raise money by selling stock. So it's *very-very* important that you understand how the stock market works. Investing your money does come with risks. So, let me reiterate how this work:

- When somebody buys stock in your company, they will own a piece of your company.
- You can decide how to cut it up (make sure you remain a majority owner (51%);
- Stock prices can rise and fall on any given day. If the demand for your product, goods, or services decrease, you can lose money.
- If you lose money, then the people who have bought stock or pieces of your company will lose money as well.
- When you make a profit your investors will make a profit as well.

If 10 people buy stock in your company, then the profit will be split among 10 people. Understand?

KIDPRENEUR Investing Tips

1) Buy low, sell high! The #1 thing investment professionals would tell you is to buy low and sell high. I would recommend that Kidpreneurs purchase stocks that are in the $5-$20 range. You can find quite a few companies that sell products that you love and use everyday. Selling high may mean that you sell something that just went up about $10-$30 in price.

2) Never fall for fake e-mails!
Gimmick e-mails claim to have a great investing deal *(act fast or else you'll miss out emails". Delete them.* First of all, that may be fraud. Many times these companies are about to go bankrupt and their stock prices are about to plummet. Last, it's illegal to tell someone when stocks are about to go good or bad.

3) Do your research!
Don't just pick one company because the name is pretty or because you think they have the lowest current price available. If you do your research and look into the company's history of sales and the products they provide, you may avoid some huge losses down the road.

4) You wont to always win!
Keep in mind that you may not always win. Sometimes you may anticipate a company's increase in stock prices, but become heart-broken when stock prices come crashing down right in your face.

5) Don't invest your money into a single stock!
You should NEVER invest all of your money into one single stock. If you invested your entire $10,000 into one stock and in the following months the price falls and doesn't rise until months later, you stand to lose some capital gains, and interest as the shares have depreciated. Now, what if you evenly distributed your $10,000 among (5) companies and (3) out of the (5) increase by twice as much in price and the other (2) just fall by no more than a few dollars. You just made a profit! The other two stocks don't really matter because three are now worth more than twice as much as they were.

Example 1

How to Read a Stock Table

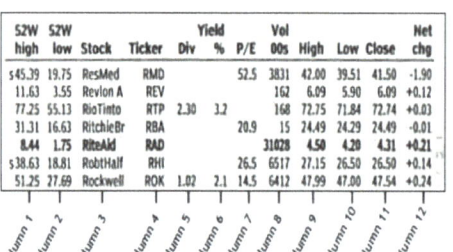

Let's take a closer look. The following is an example of the information you can find in most newspapers.

- **Columns 1&2** 52-Week Hi-Lo Range: The first two columns show the highest and lowest prices for the stock during the preceding 52-week period, not including the latest trading day.

- **Column 3** Company Name and Type of Stock: If there are no special symbols or letters following the company name, it is common stock (shares without a fixed rate of return of investment.) However, among the symbols that may commonly appear next to a company are:
    - "pf" - Indicates the listing is preferred stock (shares that generally have a fixed rate of return.) These shares of stock receive preference over common stock in the distribution of dividends.
    - "wt" - A warrant gives the holder the right to buy securities at stipulated prices, usually within a specified time limit. Popular new listings are for warrants based on advances or declines in indexes of foreign markets, such as Japan's.
    - "rt" - Indicates that stockholders have been given the opportunity (or "right") to buy new securities in proportion to the number of shares they already own, within a given time period. Since the stock offered is usually below the market value, rights have their own market and can be traded.
    - "un" - Refers to unit shares of stock, a combination of different securities that are sold together as a package.
    - "wi" "When Issued" - Indicates a conditional transaction in a security authorized for issuance but not actually issued.

- **Column 4** Ticker symbol: This alphabetic symbol uniquely identifies the stock on the exchange's "ticker" as well as many other electronic information system and computer databases.

- **Column 5** Dividend Payment: This indicates the annual dividend payment per share designated by the company for stockholders. On preferred shares, it is generally a fixed amount. On common shares, it varies with the business condition of the company is evaluated regularly by a firm's directors. When a letter follows the dividend figure, refer to the Explanatory Notes on Page C3 or C4 of the Money & Investing section of the Wall Street Journal.

- **Column 6** Percent Yield: This figure represents the dividend return an investor can expect on each share of stock. It is calculated by dividing the annual dividend each share pays by its current market value, and is expressed as a percentage.

- **Column 7** Price-Earnings Ratio (PE): This calculation is one way of evaluating a stock's relative performance and value. It is computed by dividing the stock's price by the company's per-share earnings for the most recent four quarters. Higher Price-Earnings multiples suggest the investors are more optimistic about a stock's prospects than comparable lower-PE stocks, but the reason for high and low PEs also include the company's growth outlook, the industry the company is engaged in, company accounting policies, and whether the firm is a startup or a more established business.

- **Column 8** Trading Volume: This figure shows a total number of shares traded for the day, listed in hundreds. Thus "363" would mean 36,300 shares (When a "z" precedes the volume number, the figure represents the actual number of shares traded. For example, "z20" means 20 shares, not 2,000.) Stocks with large volume surges compared with their usual activity are underlined.

- **Column 9** Hi/Lo: This indicates the trading price range of the security during the day's trading. If one of these represents a new 52-week high or low for the stock, a small up or down arrow appears to the far left of the stock's listing. The new record will be reflected in the stock's 52-week hi-lo range on the following day.

- **Column 10** Close and Net Change: The Close is the trading price recorded when the market closed on this day. If the closing prices is up or down more than 5% from the precous day's close, the entire listing for the stock is bold-faced. Net change indicates the difference between the closing price and the previous close.

Example 2

Stages, Trends, and Waves
Let's look at an example chart...

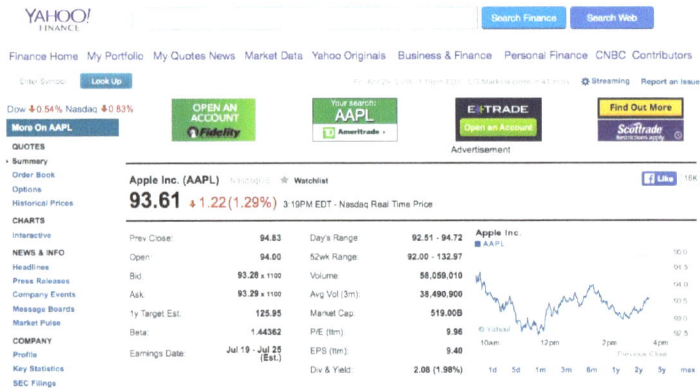

Look at the example above of preferred shares from Apple. The 1st Year Target Estimate for Apple is $125.95. If one were to go only by this projection, it would be advantageous to buy shares of Intel at the current $92.51; however, analysts are often wrong.

Day's Range
*The **day's range** specifies the lowest and highest price at which the stock has traded throughout the day.* The lowest price for Apple in this example is $92.51, while the highest is $94.72.

52wk Range`

1. The **52-week range** specifies the lowest and highest price at which the stock has traded in the past year.
2. The lowest price for share of Apple in the past year was $92.00, while the highest was $132.97.
3. Quotes in newspapers usually list the range under two separate headings: "52wk Low" and "52wk High."

If this range is extremely wide, it warrants further research. It could either mean a huge loss or a huge gain; and either way, an unpredictable, volatile stock. *Volume refers to the total number of shares traded throughout the day. Note: 58,059,010 shares in Apple exchanged hands on this day.*

KIDPRENEUR (Activity)

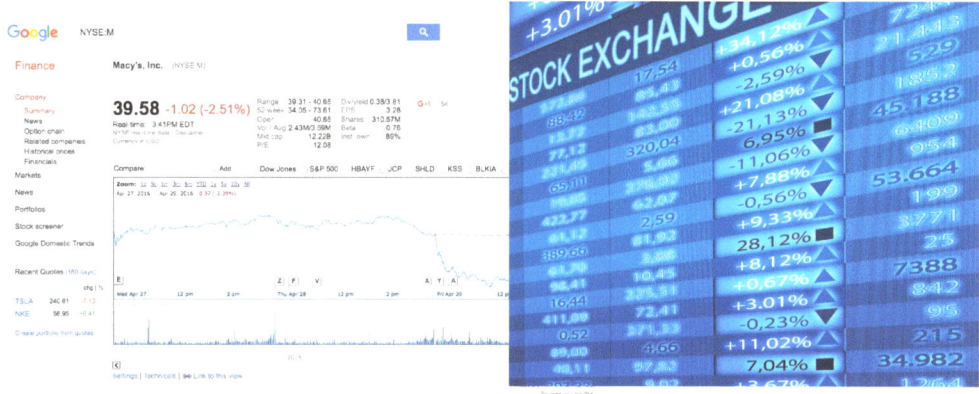

What is your favorite place to shop? Look up the symbol for the stock. What is the cost per share?

_____
_____
_____

Assignment

You have $10,000. Spend it all!
Choose not more than 5 company stocks for the 3-month period. *(Reference sites: morningstar.com, forbes.com, etrade.com, Quicken.com, wsj.com, cnnfn.com)*

1. Write in today's date_____.

2. You have $10,000 to invest. Research your stocks; make good prudent decisions.

3. Record the price when you purchased it, when you sold it and how much you made. You may re-invest your earnings, or take your money and run home smiling. On sell everything.

4. How much will your portfolio be worth in 30 days (Write the date here_____)?

5. How much will your portfolio be worth in 60 days (Write the date here_____)?

Opportunity #1 _____. I can provide _____ to _____.
　　　　　　　　　　Product/service　　　customer(s)

I can be successful because _____
_____
_____.

Opportunity #2 _____. I can provide _____ to _____.
　　　　　　　　　　Product/service　　　customer(s)

I can be successful because _____
_____
_____.

Opportunity #3 _____. I can provide _____ to _____.
　　　　　　　　　　Product/service　　　customer(s)

I can be successful because _____
_____
_____.

Opportunity #4 _____. I can provide _____ to _____.
　　　　　　　　　　Product/service　　　customer(s)

I can be successful because _____
_____
_____.

Part 3

"_____" the Kidpreneur
(insert your name)

Objectives:
- Kidpreneurs will explore real ideas for making money.
- Real life case studies of other Kidpreneurs will be studied with discussion questions following.
- Kidpreneurs will begin to learn research techniques and decision-making skills.

BASIC VOCABULARY:
Advantages
Brainstorming
Competition
Disadvantages
Influence
Prioritize
Promote
Research
Risk
Traffic count
Zoning

Real Ideas for Making Money

- **Dog Service-** open a company for walking dogs, and scooping poop *add* **Animal Boarder Services** and have people bring their pets to your home to take care of them while they are away.

- **Lemonade Stand–** Set up a lemonade stand on a busy corner on a hot day and sell lemonade. Sounds corny, but it works! Who can pass up a cute kid with a table set up on a busy corner on a summer day? The same think can be done with **hot chocolate, snow cones, or flavored popcorn.**

Car Cleaning Service
Age Requirement: 9+
Difficulty: Easy
Start-up Costs: $0 to $49
Potential Income: $10 to $20 per hour

What supplies do I need for cleaning cars? You don't need a lot of supplies for cleaning cars. In fact, you probably already have everything you need around your house. The most important part for cleaning cars is a shop vac. If you don't have one you can use your vacuum until you have saved enough money to buy a shop vac.

1. Shop-vac
2. Car cleaning rags
3. Interior Cleaning Spray
4. Exterior Cleaning Spray
5. Windex
6. Paper towels

How could you get customers for cleaning cars? Glad you ask. I would personally recommend just going door-to-door but you can always start with people you know. Work with your parent's contact list, and email. You can always handout flyers. Also you can always give a discount for getting referrals. Once you have one customer you can say, "I will give you $5 off for 5 referrals".

More Ideas for Kidpreneurs

- **Open a bakery Catering Business–** Set up a table with baked goods at a public place, garage sale or local city event.

- **Outdoor Painting Service** that specialize in Fences- Wood and metal fences need to be painted or they will rot or rust.

- **Power Washing Business-** Homes get dirty, dusty and are magnets for spider webs. Power washing the siding and eaves is really easy.

- **Gutter Cleaning Company-** Gutters will fill with leaves and debris and will clog if not cleaned. Advertise your services for cleaning gutters and consider learning how to install gutter guards.

- **Seasonal Decorator:** Installing Christmas lights- whether it's the elderly, working parents, or busy moms, by December 1st everyone needs their Christmas lights put up.

- **Holidays Decoration Installer (Up/Down Services)**- Many people go to the extreme for holiday decorating. Offer your services to help put up and take down holiday decorations.

- **Holiday Yard Flag Installer-** Many people are patriotic and love to have a national flag placed in their yard or on their home on national holidays. A Flag Install business is very original and your services could be expanded to team flags on game days.

- **Game Day Yard Flag Installer**- Most people are sports fans of one sport or another. Put their team flag up in their yard everyday there is a game.

- **Christmas Tree Disposal** Service- Carry the tree away after the season is over.

- **Air Filter Changing Business**- Change or clean air filters for heaters and air conditioners for homes.
- **Painting Service-** Set up a service to go to homes and print vinyl letters for curbs, (emergency and night time).
- **Designer**- Baby Hair Bows- Make and sell little girl hair bows to boutiques.
- **Designer-Aprons**- Make and sell aprons at local boutiques or on Craigslist.
- **Designer- Wreaths**- Make and sell wreaths to decorations shops.
- **Decorative Pillow-maker**- Make and sell decorative pillows at boutiques.
- **Designer- Earring Holder**- Make and sell earring holders out of picture frames and wire.

- **Outdoor Movie Producer**- Set up an outdoor movie in your back yard with a projector and speakers and invite the neighborhood. Charge admission and sell drinks and popcorn.
- **Can you DJ** for a local wedding or event?
- **Artist-** Face Painting- Set up a face-painting booth at a park or a local city event.
- **Tutoring business-** Open an after school tutoring business-
- **Floral Business**- sell flowers and make bouquets for special holidays right from your garage
- **Farming**- selling eggs, raise and sell piglets, feed horses, & cows, grow a herb garden and sell the goods.
- **Video Tech**- Digitalize Pictures- Many people have tons of photos in scrapbooks and boxes that are useless. Scan them into the computer to make digital copies; Do movie conversions- VHS and home videos to digital copies and DVDs; trouble shoot and help the elderly set up their email and wi-fi services.
- **Video Rental Service-** Video Game Rental- Rent out all your video games to friends for a fee.
- **Landscaping Business-** This can be a good business is you are good at changing out perennials and flower beds, maintaining yards, laying seeds, fertilizing, turning on sprinklers when neighbors are on vacation and learning how to make and sell organic pest control (BIG BUSINESS- I might do this one myself).
- **Recycling Business-** Recycle Metal- Collect aluminum cans, copper wire, or other metal and recycle for money.
- **Sell firewood**

Want to know more? Here's a site that has over 200 ideas:
https://www.youtube.com/user/howtomakemoneyasakid

Real Life KIDPRENEURS

Kid Entrepreneurs Jaden Wheeler & Amaya Selmon's 'Kool Kidz Food Truck Business

Jaden Wheeler and Amaya Selmon are the youngest food truck owners in Memphis, TN. The brother and sister team, Jaden 12, and Amaya 11, own and operate **Kool Kidz Sno Konez,** a little enterprise that started in their front yard just a few years ago.

"We were always asking my mom for stuff, because we wanted her to buy us toys and things, and she said 'Why don't y'all make your own money?'". We though about it, and did!

Jaden & Amaya loved Jerry's Snow Cones, a good drive from their southeast Memphis home, and that spurred the idea. "We started out with a card table, a blender, and an extension cord in front of our house," Jaden said.

They enlisted friends to stand at the busier streets around the neighborhood, waving signs to lure customers. Success came right away, and last summer they did the same thing, though they had an ice shaver by then. In two summers, they earned about $1,000. Their mother, Katrina Robinson, was willing to step in a help their company grow. "She came to us with the food truck idea," Jaden said.

They found an old transport van for sale on Craigslist, bought it in February (with considerable help from their Mom), had it refurbished to food truck standards and ready to go just 3 months later. The next step was to get licensed by the County Health Department. The outside was painted a bright yellow with a serving window on the side. "These kids are the youngest food truck operators in town!" said Taylor Berger, the president of the Memphis Food Truck Association.

Jaden makes the snow cones. Their Mom, a single parent, who is a registered nurse, drives the truck; and Amaya works the window. They typically work on Saturdays and Sundays, though they'll go out during the week for special events. They sell more than 20 flavors, and very recently added hot dogs and nachos to their menu. Jaden has big plans. "Our goal with the truck is to franchise it, so I don't have to work when I grow up," he said. *Not work? From a kid who started his own business when he was 10 years old?* "What I mean is that… I want to work smart instead of working hard," "he said. You can find them by following them on their Facebook page.

Discussion Questions

1. How old was Jaden and Amaya when they 1st became a Kidpreneurs?

2. Who or What influenced Jaden and Amaya to open her own business?

3. What special Kidprenuer characteristics do Jaden and Amaya have?

4. What was the risk for **Kool Kidz Sno Konez**?

5. What impressed you most about Jaden, Amaya, or **Kool Kidz Sno Konez**?

Source: http://www.africanamerica.org/topic/kid-entrepreneurs-jaden-wheeler-and-amaya-selmons-kool-idea-leads-to-food-truck-business

Kidnovation

KIDPRENEUR Activity:

SELECT 3 BUSINESSES THAT YOU BELEIVE YOU CAN BE SUCCESSFUL OPERATING. DESIGN A FLYER PROMOTING YOUR BUSINESS.

1.

2.

3.

Discussion Questions

1. WHICH ONE OF THE BUSINESSES FROM THE PREVIOUS PAGE DO YOU FEEL YOU WOULD BE BEST SUITED?

2. WHY DID YOU THINK YOU WOULD BE SUCCESSFUL?

3. WHAT WOULD YOU DO TO CAPTURE THE PUBLIC'S ATTENTION?

4. WHAT ARE YOUR QUALIFICATIONS FOR OPERATING THIS BUSINESS?

5. IS THERE A DEMAND FOR YOUR PRODUCT/SERVICE? WHY WOULD THE PUBLIC LIKE YOU / IT?

6. WHAT WILL BE THE RISK IF YOU STARTED THIS BUSINESS?

7. WHAT WILL BE THE REWARDS FOR YOU OWNING THIS BUSINESS?

Kidpreneur Interview Form

Have you thought of interviewing another successful business owner? Here is an easy form that you can use over and over:

Name of entrepreneur:

___

Name of entrepreneur's business?

___

Type of businesses organization:

___

Number of employees:

___

List the benefits to society:

___

Chart the growth since inception:

___

Challenges in operating the business:

___

KIDPRENEUR Decision Grid

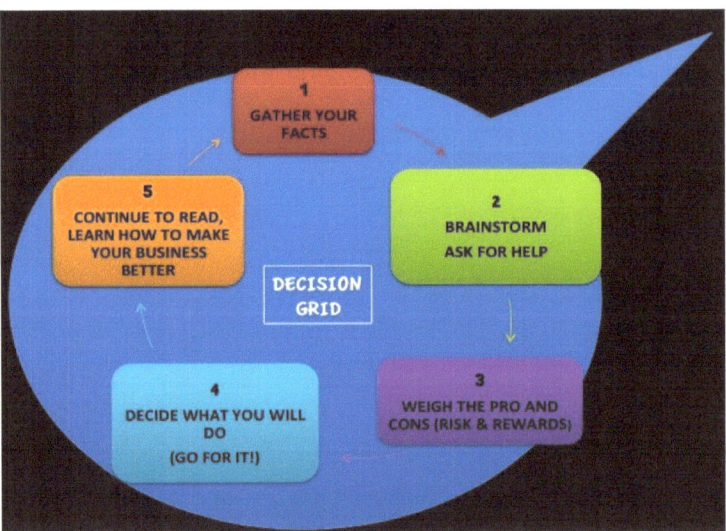

THERE ARE 5 STEPS IN THE KIDPRENEUR DECISION-MAKING PROCESS

Step 1. Now that you have identified your business venture, the first step will be to gather all the information you can about that business. How much will it cost you to manufacture your product or deliver your service? Who will your customers will be? Where will your business be located? How much profit can you make and how much profit do you need to make to stay in business?

Step 2 is brainstorming. Share all the information you collected with your parents or your business partner, and ask for help. You will need lots of good advice to get started.

Step 3: Weigh the pros and cons and evaluate the risk of opening your business. Do you have enough money to operate your business for a certain amount of time even if you don't make a profit right away? Do you need to advertise? Will you need a computer, an iPad, or a cash register?

Step 4: This is the one that I like… if everything appears as if it's going to work, get started! *Go for it and give it your best.* Try to remember that you will have to juggle your business and school homework at the same time. You may have to forgo basketball or cheerleading tryouts. Prioritize!

Step 5: You will need to use the Internet, read magazines, and visit other businesses similar to yours. Learn everything you can to make your business grow. Find ways to help you work faster while still giving good service.

Before you open!

1. Do your research. Learn everything you can about the business that you plan to open, just because Peter is good at it, does not mean Paul will be too!

2. Curb your spending to save money for your start up and operating expenses.

3. Don't try to spend all your money, or all your mom and dad's money. Have a predetermined amount that you will use to open and operate your business.

4. Make a "for" and "against" list describing your business, your competition, and the people who you plan to serve (demographics).

5. Consider the advantages of operating a family owned business.

6. Make sure you use your strengths to measure your skills, and then evaluate the training that you will need to operate successfully.

7. Take a class to overcome your short comings (accounting).

8. Before you open, test the market invite your friends and family over to sample your service or product.

9. Don't forget to check the zoning in the area. Will the County allow you to open? Will you need any special licenses or permits?

10. Consider specializing in a single product or service (keep it simple).

11. Start small to gain credibility and a loyal customer base.

12. Complete a written business plan before you start (see next chapter).

13. Spend some time doing budget planning and make a 12-month cash flow projection before you open.

14. Watch the risk! If you're 12-month cash flow statement looks speculative, you may want to wait or get some more advice before the grand opening.

15. Watch the competition if you don't think you have a chance to be successful again look at the numbers and the population that you'll be serving. Don't open the business! There's no penalty for a missed opportunity!

16. Last be patient. Nothing happens overnight and avoid anyone who comes to you with get rich quick ideas.

Others things to consider:

Traffic count: Will your business be visible to the public?	Demographics-(income & population) of the neighborhood or community?
Will people need a car to get to your location?	Staffing: How many persons will you need to operate?
Will parking be available?	Crime?
Operating hours?	The minimum wage you can pay?
Rental (lease) rates for your business location?	Will a permit (s) be required?
Signage?	Utilities?

WRITE DOWN THE NAMES OF "3" BUSINESSES THAT WILL BE SIMILAR TO YOURS.

No ideas yet, just pick 3 businesses in your community that you *think* are successful. Analyze what you think makes them successful. Make a short list here:

Notes:

Use this template for the business that you plan on opening:

"FOR" & "AGAINST" LIST

FOR	AGAINST

"…take up an idea, make that one idea your life- think of it, dream of it, live on that idea. Let the brain, muscles, nerves, every part of your body be full of that

idea, and just leave every other idea alone. This is the way to success".
Sami Vivekananda

Part 4
KIDPRENEUR Business Plan

BASIC VOCABULARY:
Benefit
Business
Budget
Cash-flow statement
Consumer
Corporation
Decision-making
Franchise
Interest rate
Invest
Legal forms of Business
Liability
Opportunity cost
Partnership
Sole Proprietor

Parts of the Business Plan:
1. The vision/mission statement (your goals)
2. Business Profile (outline your service /product
3. Your market (people who need your service/product)
4. Economic Assessment (can people afford your service/product)
5. Marketing Plan (how will you get the word out)
6. SWOT Analysis (Pro's & Con's of developing and operating your business)
7. Budget (how much money do you have to start, buy product; how much profit do you expect to make?

5 questions to ask before starting a business

Why do I want to start this business?
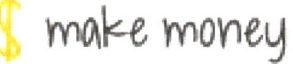 make money  do good > both?

What resources do I need?
office? shared space?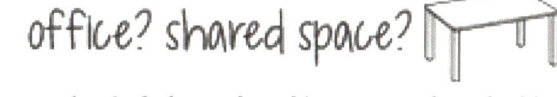

How do I fit into the rest of the world?
 unique idea?  who else has done it?

What is my business structure?
non-profit — hybrid? — for-profit

Do I have the skills & aptitude to be an entrepreneur?
 be ready to take a risk!

Developing your Business Profile
*Before you can develop your **business plan**
you have to put together a **business profile**!*

Before you attempt to write anything on paper, you want to study (research) other businesses like yours. Look at their profiles and try to understand why they are successful. While doing your research make sure you use the most accurate and up to date data that you can find. Your clients won't be interested in what you did five years ago. **They will want to know how you will deliver your service or product to them now.**

The first thing you need to do is write down the **name of your company;** second, **the year established** (*open for business*), **what your company does,** who the **principal** (*owner*) is, and all your **contact information** (*your website if you have one- Facebook, Twitter, Instagram or Snapchat names*).

For example:

Angel Artistic Expressions
2016
Angel Hope
999 Carli Way
Summerville, N.Y. 87655
Facebook, Twitter, Instagram: @angelart

The second thing is to talk about your company. If you already have your mission statement it goes right here, if not, we'll go over how to prepare one in the next few pages. This is also a good place to talk a little bit about what is driving or who is supporting you?

The third part of your company profile is to talk about what you need to run your company (organizational analysis):
- How many people do you need to work for you?
- What type of services will you provide?
- Whether you intend to use software or technology to help you deliver your product or service.
- Do you have any major accounts already?
- Is there market waiting on your product?

4. Summing this up will be the hard part. Take all of this information and condense it (make it short), still you want to be as detailed as possible. Be sure you point out the things that make you wonderful and point out the

things that will ensure *(almost guarantee)* your success. Use the chart below to list your weak areas, and get some advice on how to eliminate or minimize them:

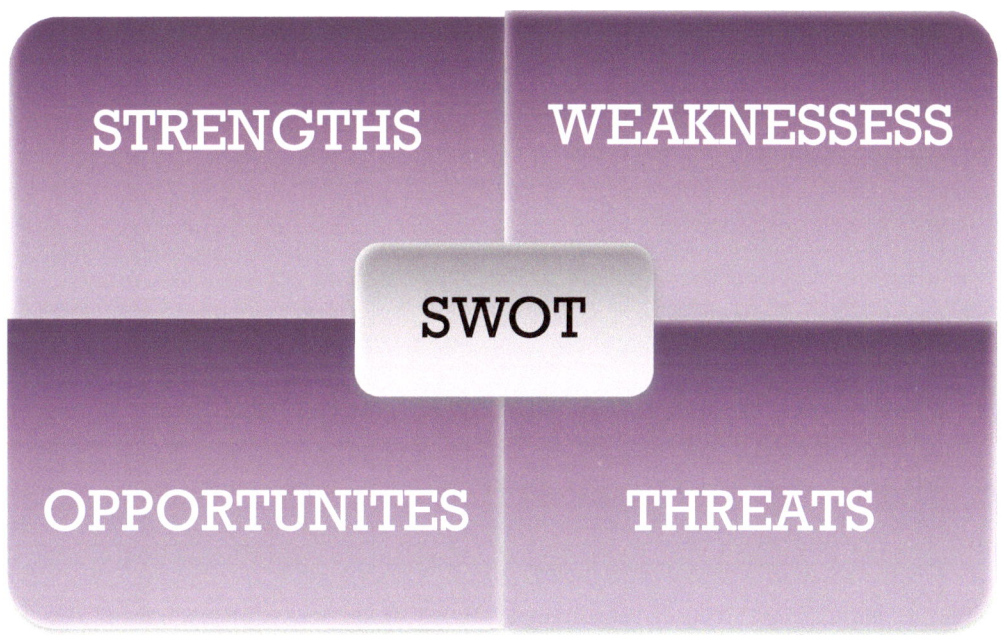

Last, you want to mention why your company will be the best! Be creative but don't exaggerate. What is your special talent? **Threats** may be other businesses just like yours in close proximity. Get a discussion going with your close friends or family and come with some ideas that will set you and your business apart from all the rest. Use the practice sheet on the next page to develop your Company Profile. Consider asking your parents or someone that's already in business to read this over before you submit it. This will be the cover sheet to your Business Plan.

Company Profile Worksheet

Name of business:
Year established:
A one line description:
Owner's name:
Owners address:
Owners phone number:
Owner's email:
Social media names:

Mission Statement:

Organizational Analysis

SWOT ANALYSIS

STREGTHS	WEAKNESSES
OPPORTUNITIES	THREATS

What is Cash Flow / Statement?

What is cash flow? Cash flow is a picture of your business in a spreadsheet. Cash flow is the money that's moving in and out of your business *(the payment for goods and services-and the money you continually use to buy more equipment to operate your business)*.

If you are earning more money than your expenses, you have a **positive cash flow.** You have enough money to pay your bills and you are making a profit. On the other hand, if you are spending more money to operate your business than what you are collecting for your goods, service, or product, you have a **negative cash flow**.

Cash flow is the reason why a lot of companies go out of business (overnight). Ever woke up and set out to shop at one of your favorite stores only to find a door locked and *a no-longer in business sign?* It's probably because they had a negative cash flow.

Cash flow is earnings before Depreciation. It is the best measure of a company's Financial health

If you want to open a seasonal business, that is, a business that revolves around holidays or seasons like a firewood yard, cash flow may be a really big problem. You will need to keep your business operating during the months when your service or product is not needed or not in top demand.

How do you analyze your cash flow? You begin with a **cash flow statement.** I'm including one on the next page. Here you will record when a customer pays you and how much cash you use for supplies, utilities, or employee wages. These are called expenses. If you need to buy equipment or pay a lease, the amount you spend will go on there too! When you starting out you need to look at this on a weekly basis, later you can analyze your cash flow on a monthly basis.

Cash Flow Statement Template

Use this template as a starter to determine your cash flow. Add more columns to extend it to a year, add more rows for expenses or for other ways you may bring "cash in." After you do your initial figures, ask yourself, "does it make sense to open this company"? If you are already open, "should I revisit my business plan, up my marketing game, or simply close the doors?"

CASH FLOW STATEMENT

	Fiscal year begins	jan	feb	mar	apr	may	june	july	aug	sept
CASH ON HAND										
Cash sales										
Total cash										
CASH PAID OUT										
merchandise										
wages										
Advertising										
supplies										
Lease (rent)										
Accounting (legal fees)										
Utilities										
Other expenses _____										

What type of Business will you have?
Corporate Structure

We are ready to open my jewelry shop. My sister and I have been busy all summer. Mom is helping with the website. What else do I need?

Now, to the fine details:

Starting a business is risky. Partnering with two or more people can be risky. There may be disagreements and power struggles on how to operate the business. There are three (3) main types of business organizations. It gets technical from here:

In the last two chapters you read stories of kids just like yourself that are running successful businesses. Almost all of them had help. Remember, **Snowconz** was a partnership (brother and sister). You should now be able to determine just how much help you will need after going through the decision grid.

You will need to decide what type of business organization will be the most advantageous for you. There are three main types of business organizations: **Sole proprietorship, partnerships, and corporations.** Many small businesses, especially Kidpreneurs operate as sole proprietor or partnerships. If you can grow that business into something really big it can potentially become a corporation.

Let's walk through some definitions. A **Sole Proprietor** is a business that's owned and managed by just one person and that person assumes all the risk and the rewards, the losses and the profits.

Sole Proprietor	Advantages	Disadvantages
	Easy, low start up cost	High liability (risks)
	Freedom to be creative	Maybe hard to raise money
	You keep all the profits	
	You have control	

A **partnership** is a business that is owned and operated by two or more people and those people assume all the risks, and losses, and share in all the profits.

Partnership	Advantages	Disadvantages
	Easy, low startup cost	High liability (risks)
	Joint decision making	Hard to find the right partner
	Shared risk(s)	Authority is divided

Corporations are more complicated. A corporation is created by law. It is a legal entity owned by two or more people. Those people are called stockholders, the difference is stockholders are only at risk for the amount of their financial investment. *Remember Chapter 2 when we talked about using stock to grow your business?*

Corporation	Advantages	Disadvantages
	Lower risk (liability)	Regulated by State/Fed laws
	Easier to raise capital	Higher taxes
		Loss of independence
		Lots of record keeping

There is one more type of business and it's called a franchise. You see those around your home cities every day. McDonald's, Smoothie King, Starbucks, Dollar General, and Burger King are just a few examples of franchise businesses. This involves almost no creativity because you buy the *business in a box*.

The parent company provides training and advertising that helps the Kidpreneur make a profit. In turn, the Kidpreneur agrees to run the business like all the operations around the country, uphold certain standards, and pay a franchise fee to the parent organization.

Franchise	Advantages	Disadvantages
	Reasonable upfront cash	Franchise fees
	Entrepreneur training	Little or no input
	Entrepreneur support	Hard to cancel the contract
	Management assistance	

KIDPRENEUR planning

Writing the Business Plan pg. 1.

A business plan is a document (much larger than any book report you ever written) that describes your business idea or the service you want to offer, and then tells how you plan to open shop. It includes your business address, who you will be selling to, how you plan to raise and spend your money, and most of all, how much profit you anticipate making. Specifically, business plans address:

- Background- What type of business?
- Mission Statement- What do you stand for? And why do you do it?
- Financial Plan- Do you plan to make a profit?
- Market Data- Who are you serving, and what benefits do you offer them?
- Outcomes- Will you solve a problem for your customers?

Think of your business plan as a road map. You will need to be as detailed as possible to attack a partner if you will need their financial help. This shows them you are committed to making your business venture a success.

1. What was the business idea you chose in Chapter 2?

_____
_____
_____

2. Do you have a **NAME for your business**? Is it easy to remember or pronounce?

_____
_____
_____

3. What type of **organization** will you be? Will you be a sole proprietor, or will you have a partner?

_____
_____

Writing the Business Plan pg. 2.

4. Have you thought about a **MISSION STATEMENT**? The mission statement will help keep you focused. It is typically (1) sentence, just 2-4 lines that answers the following questions:
   - What inspires you?
   - What will make your business unique?
   - What will your company do for its customers?
   - What will you do for your employees,

This is your opportunity to define the business goals, and make sure your decisions are aligned to your mission. Give it a try on the following lines:

_____
_____
_____

Don't worry if you it does not sound quite right the first (5) times. You can always improve it. Want to try again?

_____
_____

5. **MARKETING**
Who will your customers be? Children? Adults?
_____
_____

Where will your business be located? Will customers need a car to get to you?
_____
_____

Is your product or service expensive?
_____
_____

Writing the Business Plan pg. 3.

What will be your cost for supplies?

Describe your target customer?

Will you need technology in your business?

How will you get the word out about your business?

Will you have a Facebook or Twitter page for your business?

------

6. FINANCES

How much will it cost to start your business?

What do you need to buy to get started (materials, equipment)?

Writing the Business Plan pg. 4.

Where will you get the money? Are you using money in your saving account?

7. PRICING//PROFIT

What will be your cost for making each product? How much will it cost you in labor to provide your service?

How much will you charge for your services? How much are you selling your product for?

How much will you make on each sale after you subtract your expenses?

Sales price of item	
Cost of item	
Profit	

What will you do with the money you make? *(put it in the bank, pay employees, pay your Mom back, save for college, buy supplies)*

*Condense all this information into a **1-page Business Plan** on the next page. Make copies. Some investors will only want to see this condensed version; others will want to see the **details**. Revisit the longer version as you grow and make changes as needed.*

KIDPRENEUR 1-page Business Plan

Business Name: _____

Mission Statement: _____
_____
_____

Marketing: _____
_____
_____
_____

Who are your customers: _____
_____
_____
_____

Finances:
Start up cost _____
_____

expenses _____
_____

Contact information: _____
_____

Social media _____
_____

Check Your Understanding

Read each of the following scenarios.
Determine the profit or loss for each business idea.

Sales revenue – Expenses = Profit /Loss

Example: Steve will open his firewood business in October just in time for the fall in Denver. He is bundling 6 logs for $5. His cost is $.50 a log. The rope to tie the bundle is $.30.

- What is his cost per bundle?
- Sales revenue ($5) – Expenses ($3.30)= Profit ($1.70)
- His first order is for 5 bundles. How much will his gross sales be?
- (5 bundles x $5 = $25.00)

6. Mason's leather bracelets were a hit with all the kids in camp this summer. He now has the opportunity to have a booth at the PTA meeting at his elementary school next month. The cost for the booth is $25.00. His supplies were $37. He is hoping to sell at least 25 bracelets for $5 each. Can he make a profit at the PTA meeting?

   _____ - _____ = _____
   Sales revenue   Expenses   Profit/loss

7. 13-year-old Alexia's cookie business is doing well. With her Mom's help she is using the internet to order her baking supplies. She is having a cookie sale this weekend. She paid $9.50 for the items she needed to bake the cookies. Alexia earned $30.00 in the bake sale. Figure her profit or loss.

   _____ - _____ = _____
   Sales revenue   Expenses   Profit/loss

8. Twin brothers, Michael and Myles *Can Recycling Company* (CRC) has been open for one month. The recycling center pays $2.00 for each pound (lb.) of

aluminum. The first haul is 15 lbs. Their only cost is a $1 bag to bag each lb. of aluminum. Figure the profit or loss for this 1st transaction:

_____ - _____ = _____
Sales revenue   Expenses   Profit/loss

9. Megan's and her cousin are raking leaves in the subdivision. They printed the flyers for free at home, but the cost of the ink was $12. They paid their little brother Caleb $5 to distribute the flyers in the neighborhood. They spent $50 for their equipment, which was a loan from their Mom and Dad.

    They have raked 6 lawns in just 2 weeks. They charged $15 for small yards.

    Have they made a profit yet?

_____ - _____ = _____
Sales revenue   Expenses   Profit/loss

5. Which idea has the most revenue? _____

6. Which idea has the least revenue? _____

7. Which idea has the most expenses? _____

8. Which idea has the least expenses? _____

9. Which idea earns the most profit? _____

10. Which idea earns the least profit? _____

11. Is there any idea that loses money? _____

What did you learn? Now use this lesson to figure out your own profits:

Part 5
Business Operations

Objectives:

- Kidpreneurs will be able to determine the difference between fixed & variable costs.

- Kidpreneurs will be able to evaluate their current business opportunities for potential profits.

- Kidpreneurs will be able to identify common traits they already possess to be successful business persons.

- Kidpreneurs will be able to rate the importance of possessing some traits over others.

- Kidpreneurs will be able to define demand, and learn decision-making techniques to react if/when demand shifts.

Basic Vocabulary:
Demand
Profit
Fix cost
Variable cost
Cost of production
Kidnovation
Kidnovators
Kidpreneurship

How big is your slice of the pie?

Kids become Kidpreneur's for many reasons: the desire to earn a profit, to save up for a larger project, to fulfill a social cause, or perhaps their parents are entrepreneurs. Still others have great aspirations to become a CEO of a Fortune 500 company one day. So it's important very early that you understand the meaning of **profit, return on investment, total revenue, fix, and variable cost.**

You learned in Part 4 that **profit** is the difference between the money you earned minus the total it costs you to produce your product or deliver your service.

Fix cost is the cost of your production that stays the same every single time you buy supplies, and **variable cost** are production costs that may change from time to time. For instance, the gift boxes you bought to sell your handmade jewelry from Costco last month may be less at an online retailer this month. This change may increase your **profit.**

Your **total revenue** is your selling price multiplied by the number of items sold.

Example:

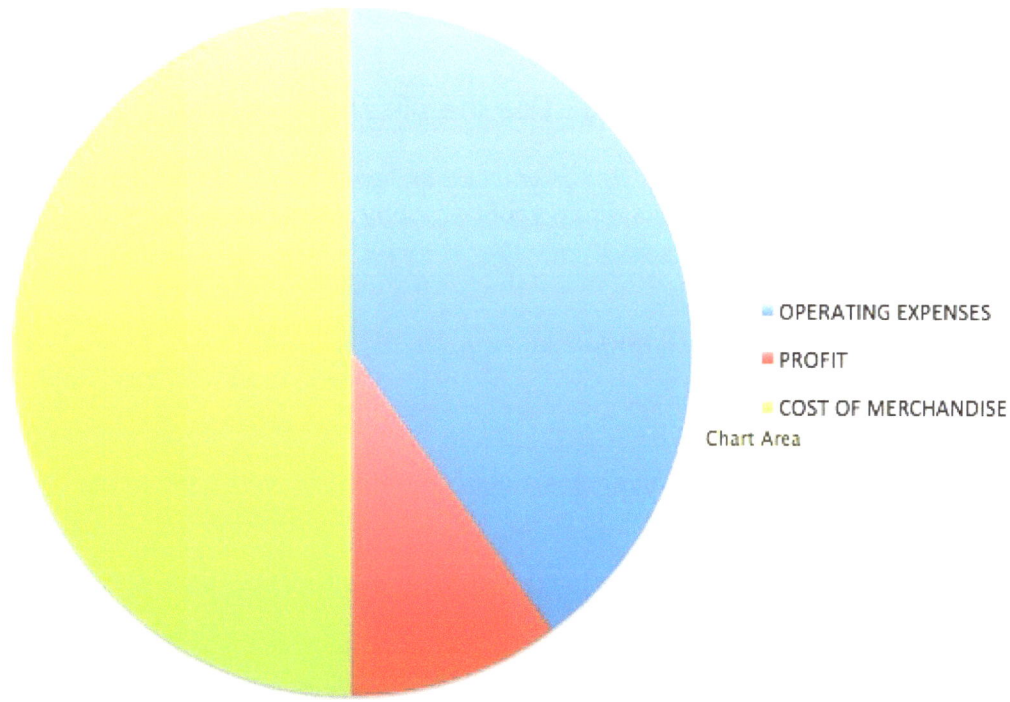

How is Your Pie Divided?

Your blank slate:

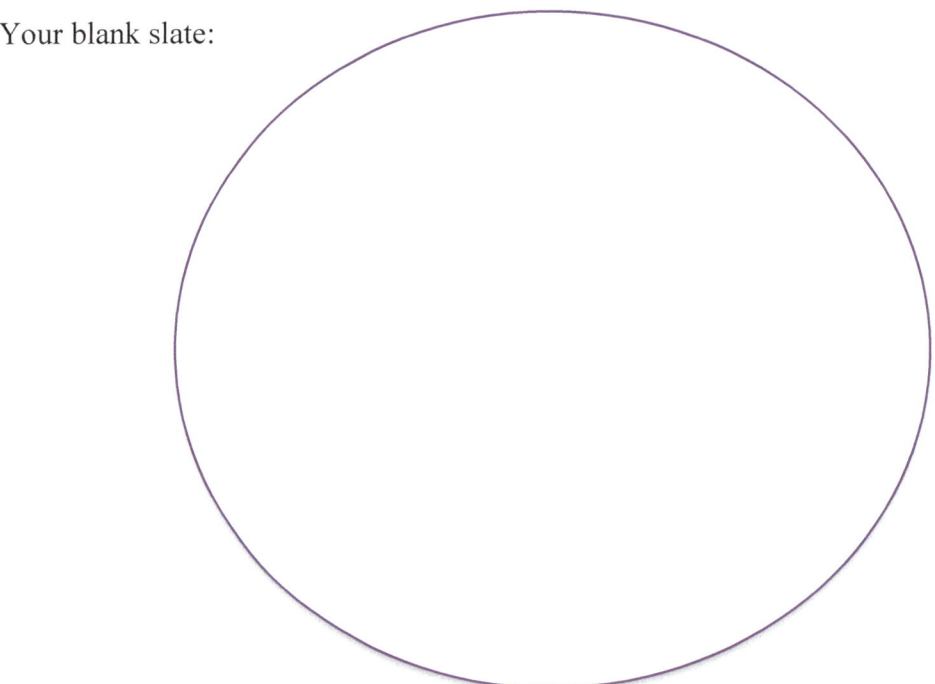

How will your pile be divided? Use the pie above as your *blank slate*.

Take another look at the company that you use to develop your business profile and your business plan in Chapter 4. From your **company sales** you will have to pay **operating cost (**salaries for people who may work for you, advertising, utilities, rent or taxes).

Estimate the **cost of your merchandise** *(supplies,* packaging). *Yikes!* To find out what your profit will be, you will have to subtract all of these expenses from your sales.

Use the pie chart above to mark off the amount of profit you will expect to earn, your operating expenses, and the cost to deliver your service or product.

Now step back and take a look at the pie chart. Share it with your parents or someone that you know and admire that owns a successful business. Do you need to make any changes? Are you satisfied with the numbers? Are you able to save money in any area? You can adjust and re-adjust the lines as many times as needed.

Understanding Fixed and Variable Cost

Maurice's Cakes and Sweets has been open for 6 months now. With the help of his father, who is also a great baker, 16-year-old Maurice has been putting in about 20 hours a week over the Summer fulfilling orders. At the end of this Summer he looked at his profit and was terribly disappointed. He is now reworking his business plan to increase his **profit margin**

Study the data below and answering the questions, can you help Maurice:

Cupcake sales (6 months)	$525.00	
Baking Equipment	75.00	fixed
Advertising (flyers)	15.00	fixed
Insurance	75.00	fixed
Salary to part – time helper	35.00	variable
IPad for taking credit card payments (refurbished)	225.00	fixed
Uniforms	25.00	fixed
Cupcake supplies	30.00	variable

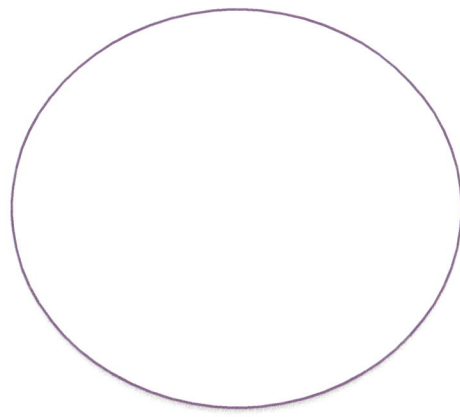

Draw the lines: Identify the profit, operating expenses, and the cost of merchandise to start *Maurice's Cakes and Sweets.*

How do you think Maurice and his Dad should account for their time and labor?

3. Should Maurice stay in business? Is there any advice for this Kidpreneur?

Dr. Danette O'NealKidpreneur 101

Kidpreneur Activity
Projecting your Profits

Your Mom is President of your Basketball's Booster Club. They are trying to raise money for new uniforms. A proposal (business idea) has been submitted to the other parents to run the concession stand during the games this season. There are 10 games this season. Your Mom believes The Bulldogs can sell 75 BULL-dogs (hotdogs) per game at $2.00 each, and 75 bags of chips for $.50 and 100 cans of soft drink for $1.00 each. $50.00 will have to be given to the school each game day for the custodian. The parents will work the concession stand, so labor will be free.

Check the prices at your local grocery to compute the supply and operating cost of the Concession stand for the season. Complete the expense statement, indicate whether the expense is fixed or variable:

	Total cost supplies	Projected profit	Fix/viable
Concession stand rental for 10 games	$2,000		Fixed
Hot dog buns (75 per game)			
Hot dogs (75 per game)		1500	
mustard			
ketchup			
napkins			
paper plates			
can drinks	1	1,000	
chips		375	
ice			
Total cost	$	$2875.00	

Take a look at the cost of supplies and the **projected profit** you can earn opening the concession stand for the Basketball Booster Club. Will you make a profit? Is it worth all the work for 10 games? Should the Booster Club try to do something else as a fundraiser?

Notes:

Comparing Gross Revenue & Net Profit

Eric was excited. His growth income from his jewelry making business was $406 for the entire summer. He received a start-up gift of $100 from his Mom. He spent $20 to purchase more capital equipment and had $130 in expenses. What is Eric's net profit?

ACCOUNTING WORKSHEET		
Starting revenue		$100.00
Sales	+	
Gross revenue		
Capital equipment	−	
subtotal		
Expenses	−	
NET PROFIT		

Marcus's Brownie sales totaled $446.85. His Dad gave him $50 to get started. He spent $30 on capital equipment and had $75 in expenses. Admittedly the expenses were a little high because the brownies are made from all organic ingredients. Marcus also paid his little brother Mark $25 for helping. What is Marcus's net profit?

ACCOUNTING WORKSHEET		
Starting revenue		$50.00
Sales	+	
Gross revenue		
Capital equipment	−	
subtotal		
Expenses	−	
NET PROFIT		

Who had the largest gross revenue?_____

Who had the largest net profit? _____

Kidpreneur Comprehension
Projecting Profit

*"Whoever said the sky is the limit, didn't know there were footprints on the moon..."
Most people set goals based on what other people think they should do. You have to love the result more than the pain it takes to get there".*

Entrepreneurs and Kidpreneurs alike, often over estimate their profits because:
- either they don't keep records of their sales,
- they don't consider the value of their time, or
- they don't know how to control their labor cost.

If you open a business and are not earning a profit:
- You should close the business and put your money in the bank.
- Try to merge your company with another profitable business, or
- Lower your prices so you can sell more items, thereby making a profit?

Lisa age 18, of *Lisa's Courier* has been making deliveries for the InTown family owned drugstore for two years now. She delivers to elderly and sick people who can't make their way into the city to pick up their medicine on Saturdays and Sundays. She averages about $105 each week including tips. In just one year she has save $4500 and wants to buy her own car. She's been using her Dad's car for deliveries.

If Lisa buys her own car, then she can expand her services to include evenings after she gets out of school. She can also pick up another customer, an office building in the same block that needs courier services.

Lisa believes that this is a wise investment. Write a brief essay that explains why Lisa may be right or wrong. (Hints are on an *Answer Page* in the Appendix).

Essay:

Kidnovation

Kidnovation is the willingness and ability to do something that no one else has tried. **Inventing** is when you are creating something that satisfies or solves a problem. It is an idea to create something to meet a challenge or satisfy a want or need. Some of you may already be Kidnovators, still other may grow up to become very famous and wealthy Kidnovators. Money is important. Possessing certain traits and characteristics are important too- **Kidnovation** requires independence, and requires you to be responsible, goal orientated, creative, confident and willing to take some risk. The most important thing of all is that you have to believe in yourself.

In either case, you need to know the difference between a *Kidpreneurs opportunity* and a *Kidpreneur idea*.

Innovation is really the driving force behind the 21st-century. Have you noticed the TV commercials lately? They're all about modernization or some original idea to capture our attention and money. In some cases, the inventor and the entrepreneur can be the same thing. Kidpreneurs invent things as a tool to effect change, to do some type of good, or to fill a void in society. They develop products, services, and products that are wanted by other people.

A **Kidpreneur opportunity** is a situation or condition favorable for attainment of a goal; a chance, or prospect or an advancement or success (www.dictionary.com).

An **Kidpreneur idea** is an excellent or ambition, a philosophy, an impression, opinion, intent or plan or action.

Read the list of traits below and rank them from 1 to 5 as to how important you think they are to **Kidpreneurship**.

Which traits do you have and which ones do you need to work on? Most of these attributes can be developed through education, training, experience, apprenticeships, and role modeling.

Kidnovator Traits

1. Look at the list of traits below needed for **Kidpreneurship** and **Kidnovation**. Kidpreneurs typically have a unique set of traits that set hem apart from other youths their same age. <mark>Check the appropriate box if you believe you already have some of these, or need to work on developing some of these traits.</mark>

Traits	Got it?	Need to work on it?	Ranking
Self confidence			
Patience			
Risk taker			
Creative			
Well organized			
Sell sufficient			
Competitive			
A leader			
Versatile (can do several things good)			
A team player			
High energy			
Seek education opportunities			
A good listener			
Determination			

<mark>2. Now pick the top 5 traits you believe to be very-very important. Rank them from 1-5 here.</mark>

1.	
2.	
3.	
4.	
5.	

If you ranked *self-confidence* as #1 you were *right on it*! Believing in yourself will get you through the bad days, and challenges of operating your own business.

Last, a Kidpreneur must be passionate about his/her business, be goal oriented crave learning, adaptable to change, and have a good understanding of **Money Matters 101** (hint). While money is important, and will serve as a barometer for your success, the characteristics that you ranked 1-5 will be far more important in helping you reach your goals.

Determining Demand

We need to spend a little time talking about demand. Assuming that you have a really good idea for a fantastic business that will make you a lot of money. Ask yourself these seven (7) questions:
- How do you know the public will like it too?
- Is there a need for it (product or service) in your community or neighborhood?
- Where will you open your business?
- Will your product work there?
- Will you have enough foot traffic (walkers) to your store or your stand?
- Are you the inventor of a *fad (something new and trending)*?
- How long will the *Fad* stay relevant?

Consumers can be very *wishy-washy* and what's popular this year may not be popular the next. Finally, can the public or community that you're serving afford your prices? *(Can you sell your snowballs for $4.25 at the kiosk you rented at the beach, but only for $2.75 in your neighborhood?)* These are all really good questions that you must consider now. Do you need to go back and change your business plan?

> Let's get some practice with a little exercise. Find a recent newspaper or magazine. Locate an ad or coupon for a hair product and a food product.

Hair Ad/ coupon:

Food product/coupon:

What is appealing about the products?

Hair Ad   **Food Ad**

How much does the product cost now?

Hair Ad   **Food Ad**

In your opinion, what is the demand for this product?
     Hair Ad   **Food Ad**

Do the math, if the prices of these products increase by 4%, would the public still by it?
  Hair Ad = price increase $_____ **Food Ad** = price increase $_____

Do you think these products will still be a demand for this product in 2 years?
     Hair Ad   **Food Ad**

<u>Use the graph to help you figure out what price you can charge:</u>

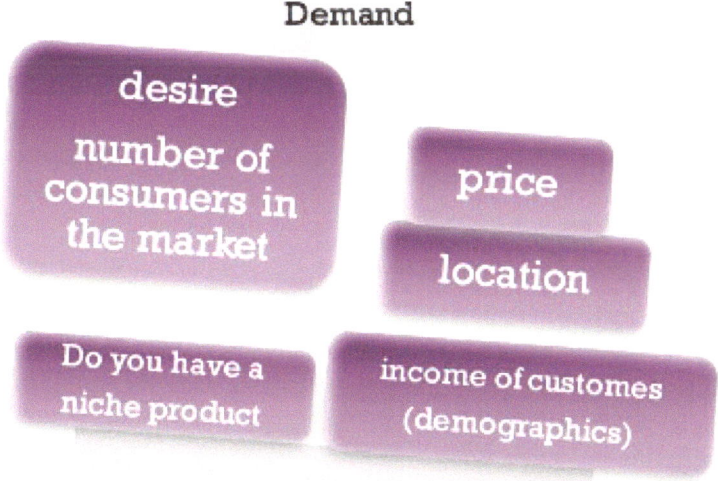

Creating Demand

Remember Lisa the courier? Another year has past she's now 19. With her parent's help, she bought a good used car that has not given her much trouble. The business is now 2 years old. Lisa expanded her business to the Mom & Pop grocery store in-town. Many seniors cannot get out to get some of the basic things needed for cooking and cleaning. The courier service now runs 6 days a week. Her brother helps on Wednesdays and Saturdays.

Lisa is admired by all, and has become quite the town-hero for the elderly. The owner of the Drug Store's brother tried to fill in last year for a week while Lisa was on vacation and it was a disaster. Lisa is thinking about restructuring her business to a fee base service. She is still only making $105 from the grocery plus tips, she gets $7 per delivery from lawyers' office, and deliver groceries for tips only. She is loosing money and working harder, not to mention gasoline has gone up from $2.30 gallon to over $3.00 a gallon this year.

1. Is there still a demand for Lisa's services?

2. Will Lisa have any risk in raising her prices?

3. Can the risk be overcome? How?

4. What can Lisa do to work more efficiently?

Lisa is working on a flyer to advertise her new fee structure. This will allow her to bring her brother on from 6-8 p.m. during the week, and for 6 hours on Saturdays. She will pay him a flat $8 per hour. Lisa is also working on a restructuring of her own hours so that she can take 2 days off a week, and have more time for studying. Should Lisa be charging more per delivery? How important is Lisa's courier service to the drug store or lawyer's office? Use the next page to design the flyer:

Discussion / Activity

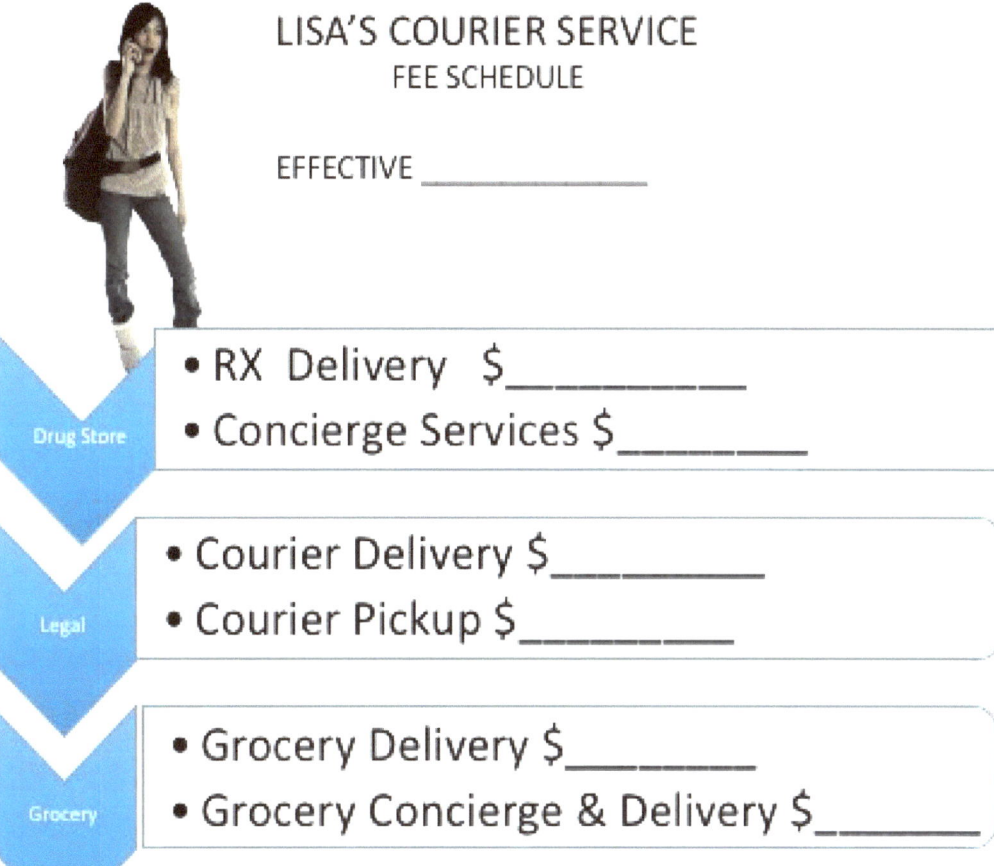

Notice that Lisa has also added a line for **Concierge Services.** You may have seen a *Concierge Desk* when your parent's checked in the last hotel, or noticed an ad in your local paper. You can now find Concierges everywhere: in hospitals, malls, in corporate buildings, apartment buildings, office buildings, airports, and now large grocery chains.

Lisa has been picking up items from the grocery and drug stores (personal shopper) for the elderly since she was 16 years old. This was the foundation that her courier business was built on. Concierge serves are becoming popular all over the United States, as some people are to just too busy to shop for dinner much needed items. In this case, Lisa stands to make a lot of money officially advertising concierge (personal shopper) services.

`

How Will You Use Your Money?

SPEND	SAVE	SHARE
$	$	$

How will you use your money?
- You will need some to buy more supplies with the money you earn.
- You learned in *Money Matters 101* that you should save at least 10% of your profits; and
- Perhaps share another 10% with your favorite charity.

I. First you will need to list your short term goals?

II. Second, list your long-term goals? What are you saving for?

III. Do you have a favorite charity that you want to give to? Do you tithe?

V. Use the graph below as a template. Add the results to your business plan.

SPEND	$	SAVE	$	SHARE	$

Cost Related Terms

A **cost savings** refers to a cost (expense) already incurred, or being paid. If Lisa (the owner of the Courier Service) trades her currently owned used vehicle for a small SUV, while maintaining the same driving habits, the driver can expect a cost savings, because she will be able to accept larger deliveries or make less trips.

An **avoided cost** is also a cost savings, but the reference is to a cost (expense) not yet incurred. After looking at your cash flow statement you decided that adding another snowball machine to the stand, *may break the bank!* Extending your operating hours by just 1 hour each day, may bring in more profit.

One of the most important things that I want you to understand is *that you can have your cake and eat it too!* Have you ever heard of *carpe diem*? It means seize the day! What do I mean by this, *"well, once you get that fantastic idea, you got to give it 200%. As you grow older you will learn that many opportunities will come once in a lifetime"*!

So let's spend a few minutes talking about **opportunity cost.** Understanding the concept of opportunity cost is critical for good decision-making. You need to learn how to evaluate risk and then decide whether not the risk is worth taking.

Part 6
Managing the Business

Objectives:
- Kidpreneurs will learn interview techniques, and hiring practices needed to operate their business.
- Kidpreneurs will learn the difference between an independent contractor and hiring an employee.

Basic Vocabulary:

Workers, Employees & Independent Contractors

It's time to hire your workforce. Yes, more things to learn… hang in there!

Your success with finding, hiring, training, and keeping your workers motivated will play a key role in your cash flow and the long-term success of your business. Payroll can be your largest expense, so you have to think carefully about the hours that you're going to be open and how many people you will need to operate your business.

Starting off with family members will be easy. You will not have to be concerned with a lot of technicalities and learning other things like payroll taxes, Social Security, income withholding taxes and Medicare expenses as deductions.

Your Workforce

Let's talk a moment about the two types of workers: employees and independent contractors. An **independent contractor** is a worker who you would pay a pre-agreed flat fee or hourly wage to complete a task. You don't have to worry about withholding deductions **(employee),** or learning about all those complicated things that adults deal with every day such as taxes. It will be the worker's responsibility to file his/her own taxes and pay any taxes on his or her earnings.

On the other hand, if your business venture turns out to be a really big enterprise, then it will come with all the complexities that corporate businesses deal with every day. You will need a lawyer, accountant, a handbook that outlines job descriptions, a benefits package, and maybe even a payroll service. Oh boy!

Preparing for the Interview

Let's talk about the interview process. Remember, in **Money Matters 101** I gave a list of interview questions and possible responses. Those were suggested to prepare the job applicant. As the boss, you now have to design your own questions. Decide first what type of person you would want working for you: energetic, friendly, able to make decisions, and competitive are just a few characteristics to consider.

1. Write a job description that clearly outlines the task and responsibilities of each position that you have an opening for. Be very detailed get some you can get some help by looking at other ads in the newspaper or online at recruiting sites.

2. Decide on the hours that you're going to need this person to work and put in your advertisement as well.

3. Review your draft, and begin thinking abut a probationary period and how you will evaluate your workers. You will want to have this handy if you decide to hire the person.

4. Set goals. Prepare your interview questions. Don't forget to include some problem solving and conflict resolution questions. Be sure you are ready to handle situations if your worker later mishandles something important while on the job.

5. You need to schedule regular training and staff meetings.

6. Recordkeeping is a must! By now you have collected a lot of paper. Grab some boxes, labels for your folders, and keep all your documents neatly filed so that you can refer back to them from time to time. Maybe there's an old file cabinet hanging around in the garage. Ask your parents can you have it. If not, large open boxes will do just fine.

7. Last, there are some other things to consider that adults deal with every day such as paid vacations, medical leave, insurance, healthcare: dental or vision plans; but, we won't get into that right now.

Remember you are on the hot-seat too! People want to work for a great company, a place where they will learn while having fun. Review and finalize your **1-page company profile** that you prepared in Part 3. Make a few copies, turn it into a flyer and add pictures if you have time. Give this to the potential employee prior to the interview. Tout your own horn. Talk about your goals, skills, experience, education, and other qualifications, especially those that match the job description and company profile well.

Sample Interview Questions

Below are a few samples of the more common types of interview questions. Write some of your own responses, and practice asking these sample interview questions aloud.

1. Tell me about yourself?

2. Why do you want to leave your current job? Why did you leave your last job?

3. What are your strengths, why would you be a good fit for this position?

4. Which adjectives would you use to describe yourself?

5. What are your weaknesses, and what are you doing to overcome them?

6. What qualifies you for this job?

7. What past accomplishments gave you satisfaction?

8. What makes you want to work hard?

9. What type of work environment do you like best?

10. Why do you want this job?

11. How do you handle pressure and stress?

12. Explain how you overcame a major obstacle.

13. Where do you see yourself five, ten or fifteen years from now?

Part 7
Financing

Basic Vocabulary:
asset
balance sheet
banker
bartering
credit
credit file
collateral
current assets
current liabilities
equity
fixed assets
fixed liabilities
income statement
lender
profit and loss statement,
secured loans
unsecured loans

In this section we will talk about financing your business. Most of you will be getting money from your parents to start your small business, but as your business grows you need to know more about how to find money to expand.

Financing Your Business

I'm assuming by now your business is up and running and the initial start up money came from your parents or someone in the family who wanted to see you succeed. They looked at your **business plan** and thought that you really had a good idea. Now it's time to expand. Going to the bank to borrow money is not as easy as you think. Most banks will not loan money to new businesses. One of the bankers' primary concern is whether not you have the ability to repay the loan for the entire amount and for the length of time that you agreed.

And **unsecured loan** is one in which someone loans you money or equipment and they basically do it with a handshake. Nothing is required of you as **collateral.** If you do not repay the loan, the lender looses and cannot recoup the losses.

A secured loan has **collateral.** The collateral is often immovable or movable property that you own and that you can pledge against the loan *(the lender holds something of value to you until you pay the loan back).*

Example: Let's say for instance you want to expand your Snowball Stand. You already own 2 snowball machines that are in really good condition, and you want to buy a 3rd. The 3rd machine is a really nice up-to-date model and can outperform the other two that you have. It is also more expensive. The cost of this machine is $2,400, you don't have that much money in your bank account, but you can make monthly payments of $75 until it's paid out. Well, the supplier may want you to give something of value for him to hold, so that you'll keep your word and pay him back. This 'something' is called **collateral**. The **lender** may require you to **pledge** your other two machines that you already own. This is his security. If you skip a payment, or you do not pay him as a promised, he not only can take his machine back, but he can also take the other two machines that you have owned for very long time. This is called **repossession.**

Don't be discouraged if you don't have a lot of money to start-up. Many businesses can be started with no money at all. You can start small and grow it with one client at a time. Almost every business that I opened, I did so with very little cash, but I had a good **Business Plan**, and projected **Cash Flow Statements.** I was passionate about my goals, and *'I was a great talker'!*

Your personal savings is *very-very* important too! Now, would be a good time to revisit the **Money Matters 101 section in Part 2.** If you haven't started already, *begin* saving and accumulating cash *now*! Find ways to stretch the money that you already have. Again, cash flow is *very very* important you will need to:
- buy supplies,
- restock your inventory,
- get a computer,
- buy equipment,
- have cash for payroll, and
- possibly cover your monthly lease.

Take a moment and think about how you will prioritize this.

> **Equity**, is the value of a thing minus any money you may owe on it. Your equity is your ownership interest. The more equity you have in the business the more cash flow you will have, and the better your **balance sheet** will look (we'll get into balance sheets a few pages later).
>
> **Equity= asset-liability**

There are 3 types of statements that are general to accounting. The **Cash-flow Statement**, the **Balance Sheet** and the **Income Statement**. At some point you will be using all three (3) if you can grow your business into an empire. For right now, I will give you just a snapshot at all three and a template to practice on.

Balance Sheet

A **balance sheet** is a financial statement that summarizes a company's assets, liabilities, and shareholders' equity at a specific point in time. The Balance Sheet gives investors an understanding and outline as to what the company owns and owes *(Investopedia.com)*. You can think of it like a snapshot of what the business looked like on that day in time.

Current Assets may include:
- Cash
- Accounts Receivable: money owed to the company by a client or customer
- Inventory: any products or materials that have already been created or acquired for the purpose of sale

Fixed Assets may include:
- Supplies: equipment used for business operations (computers, office furniture, company cars, etc.)

- Property: any office building or land owned by the business
- Intellectual property such as patents, copyrights, or trademarks.

Current Liabilities may include:
- Accounts Payable: money owed by a business to its suppliers or partners
- Business Credit Cards
- Taxes: any federal and state taxes owed for one year
- Wages: employee compensation and health insurance, etc.
- Unearned Revenue: revenues collected in advance for a service or product that has yet to be delivered to the customer.

Fixed Liabilities may include:
- Long-Term Mortgages and expenses
- Car Loan plus insurances costs)

Template

Source: http://quickbooks.intuit.com

Balance Sheet

[Date]
(all numbers in $000)

ASSETS		LIABILITIES	
Current Assets		**Current Liabilities**	
Cash		Accounts payable	
Accounts receivable		Short-term notes	
(less doubtful accounts)		Current portion of long-term notes	
Inventory		Interest payable	
Temporary investment		Taxes payable	
Prepaid expenses		Accrued payroll	
Total Current Assets		**Total Current Liabilities**	
Fixed Assets		**Long-term Liabilities**	
Long-term investments		Mortgage	
Land		Other long-term liabilities	
Buildings		**Total Long-Term Liabilities**	
(less accumulated depreciation)			
Plant and equipment			
(less accumulated depreciation)		**Shareholders' Equity**	
Furniture and fixtures		Capital stock	
(less accumulated depreciation)		Retained earnings	
Total Net Fixed Assets		**Total Shareholders' Equity**	
TOTAL ASSETS		**TOTAL LIABILITIES & EQUITY**	

Income Statement

> **The Income Statement** and the **Profit and Loss Statement (P & L)** are the same thing. *Cash flow* can be tricky and give you a false perception of how well or how poorly your business is doing. The *income statement* is a recap of your company's income and expenses over a specified period of time. This can be monthly, quarterly or annually.
>
> *Net income (or loss) = (revenue + gains) – (expenses + losses)*

Revenue on the income statement is reported when the goods or services have been provided to the customer or client (*note there is a difference in how you report here and on the Balance Sheet*).

Your expenses are the moneys that you spent to produce the **revenue.** The expenses are separated into different categories. This will help you understand exactly where your cash is going or help you better see how your money is being spent.

Operating expenses: include payroll, supplies, rent, utilities, insurance, advertising or legal fees.

Non-operating expenses: may include items like the interest you pay on money you may have borrowed for your business.

Losses: may include customer refunds, products that you messed up while trying to fulfil a service or an order, or equipment that may be stolen, etc.

Study the sample **Income Statement** below, use the template to prepare your own:

Paul's Guitar Shop, Inc. Income Statement For the Year Ended December 31, 2015		
Revenues		
Merchandise Sales	$ 24,800	
Music Lesson Income	3,000	
Total Revenues:		$ 27,800
Expenses		
Cost of Goods Sold	10,200	
Depreciation expense	2,000	
Wage expense	750	
Rent expense	500	
Interest expense	500	
Supplies expense	500	
Utilities expense	400	
Total Expenses:		14,850
Net Income		$ 12,950

Preparing the Income Statement

Income Statement

[Name]
[Time Period]

Financial Statements in U.S. Dollars

Revenue
- Gross Sales
- Less: Sales Returns and Allowances
  - **Net Sales** — 0

Cost of Goods Sold
- Beginning Inventory
- Add:
  - Purchases
  - Freight-in
  - Direct Labor
  - Indirect Expenses
- Inventory Available — 0
- Less: Ending Inventory
  - **Cost of Goods Sold** — 0

Gross Profit (Loss) — 0

Expenses
- Advertising
- Amortization
- Bad Debts
- Bank Charges
- Charitable Contributions
- Commissions
- Contract Labor
- Depreciation
- Dues and Subscriptions
- Employee Benefit Programs
- Insurance
- Interest
- Legal and Professional Fees
- Licenses and Fees
- Miscellaneous
- Office Expense
- Payroll Taxes
- Postage
- Rent
- Repairs and Maintenance
- Supplies
- Telephone
- Travel
- Utilities
- Vehicle Expenses
- Wages
  - **Total Expenses** — 0

Net Operating Income — 0

Other Income
- Gain (Loss) on Sale of Assets
- Interest Income
  - **Total Other Income** — 0

Net Income (Loss) — 0

Credit Reporting

Last, you need to keep your credit good. You can establish credit by paying people back who have loaned you money. For example, if you need to order a sign for your company, and do not have all the money to pay for it at one time, you can can ask the vendor if he offers financing. This is a great way to build a **credit file.** You can also establish credit by simply paying your utilities and your rent on time. Don't forget **bartering** is still a good way to start out! You may be able to find the equipment you need by trading off another service. *Be creative and save money!*

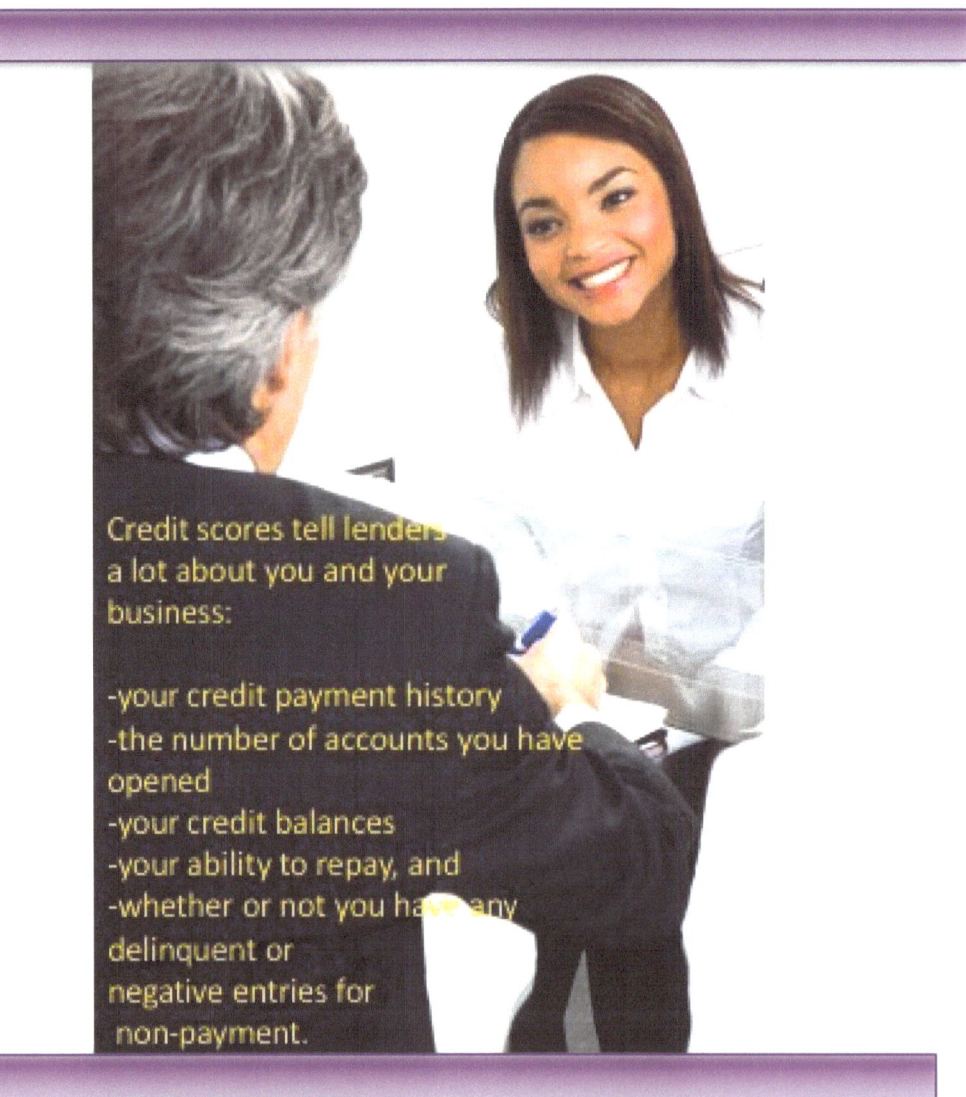

Credit scores tell lenders a lot about you and your business:

- your credit payment history
- the number of accounts you have opened
- your credit balances
- your ability to repay, and
- whether or not you have any delinquent or negative entries for non-payment.

*You probably never heard of the term **FICO** (Fair Isaac Company). FICO is the company that gathers the credit information for everyone in the world, and analyzes it to make predictive analyses. In other words, it is the **credit bureau**. Scores can range from a 400 which is not good, to a high that's over 800 which is considered an excellent score.*

Right now, if you can keep your numbers at 680 or above, you can score a homerun with your creditors. You will need to monitor this score often. You can also visit *www.myfico.com* to learn more about credit scores and credit ratings.

Establishing Credit

As Kidpreneurs, you will be building your credit file/ score from scratch. The three (3) credit bureaus are **Equifax**, **Experian** and **TransUnion**. If you want to know some quick ways to establishing credit the first would be to get a **secured credit card**. You can find these in every market and information online; but, I would strongly suggest going to one of the local banks in town that offer the card. Here's how it works:

- You deposit a certain amount of cash upfront in a savings account and the bank will issue you a credit card for the same amount. That will be your credit line or limit. You can use the card like any other credit card to buy things, and of course, pay for supplies. The most important thing is your cash deposit while earning interest in the bank is being held as **collateral.** If you do not make your payments on time, the bank can take the money in your savings account to recoup their losses, and you will have a negative entry in the credit bureau. This defeats the purpose of getting a secured card in the 1st place!
- If you pay on time, typically after a year or two, the collateral will be released, and your credit will be good enough for you to qualify for an **unsecured card**. This will result in a positive entry in the credit bureau. Read more at on this topic by visiting *www.NerdWallet.com*. This company regularly reviews and ranks secured credit card options.

The second way you can establish credit really fast is to ask your parents or an older sibling to add you as an authorized signer on one of their cards.

You can also get credit for the rental/lease payments you pay. This is the third and easiest way to obtain credit. Ask your landlord to report your rental payment history to *www.rentalkarm.com* or *www.renttrack.com*. They both report to the credit bureau. Your timely monthly lease payments history can help help you firmly establish a good credit history.

Keeping Good Credit

Keeping a good credit score (credit-worthiness) begins with developing good habits. Allow at least 6-12 months for this process.

1. Pay your bills on time- ALL OF THEM! If not, the company you owe not only will submit a negative mark on your credit, but you will lose points that may be hard to regain for at least a year; not to mention, you will begin to receive calls from a collection agency.

2. Watch how you spend. Keep your debt low enough, that you can pay some of it off if you chose each month.

3. Don't open too many accounts. Once you establish at least 2 **trade lines** (credit accounts), there will be more offers in the mail, and you will be approached at the check out counter of every major department stores. Resist! This will lower your score, even if you pay them on- time.

4. Keep accounts open for as long as possible. Unless one of your unused cards has an annual fee, you should keep them all open and active for the sake of your length of payment history and credit utilization.

5. Make it a habit at least 4 times a year (quarterly) to check each of your credit reports annually for errors and discrepancies. It happens to more people than you think. Welcome to being a grown-up!

Meeting with the Banker

Be sure you are well prepared when meeting with your bank or equity partner!

- Be prepared to answer questions about your business.
- Highlight your personal characteristics and the traits that make you good at what you do.
- Speak from your 1-page business plan.
- Bring your cash flow statement, any projections, or your balance sheet.
- Be prepared to tell the bank or your equity partners why you need the money.
- Be very specific. Give details, so they can understand the passion you have for your business.
- If you need a loan for 6 months, ask for 12 months to be on the safe side.

You'll be surprise, some investors overlook your lack of experience or lack of funds and will make a loan to you because of your passion and drive. Others will look to your grades, previous work history, or your equity partners and make a decision.

Time to pull out the Decision Grid again:
Phase 1- Decision Grid

Phase 2 (Decision Grid)

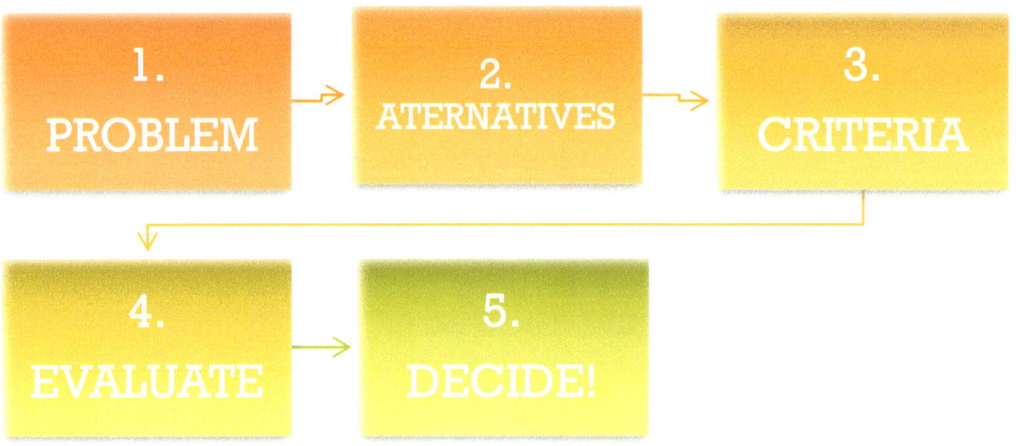

1. State the Problem
2. Consider al the alternatives to solve the problem
3. List all the the important things to consider to make a decision
4. Evaluate each alternative
5. Make a decision based upon steps 1- 4

Prepare a list of obstacles that you may have in getting start-up funding or expansion funding:

Notes:

Decision Grid

1. **Problem or Issue:**

2. **Consider the Alternatives:**

3. **List the Criteria:**

4. **Evaluate the Alternatives:**

5. **Decision:**

Funding Sources

There are other sources besides the bank where you can get money, but most will want to know the same thing: Can you pay the loan back? Here are some other sources that you may or may not be familiar with:

Friends and Family- www.virginmoney.com can help you manage the process of borrowing from people you know to ensure all parties involved are comfortable with the transaction and confident that your loans will be paid back on time.

Angel Equity Partners (ever watch Shark Tank). These persons will invest in your business in exchange for a share in ownership.

Credit Unions operate like banks, only a little more lenient.

State and City governments offer small grants for community economic development.

Venture Capital- Venture capitalist are investors that loan money to startups (small businesses) with perceived long-term growth potential. This form of raising money is very popular as new businesses do not yet have the credit required to go to the traditional bank (*another case why the* **Business Plan** *is so important*). The Venter Capitalist takes a great risk (gamble), for a potential high rate of return in the future. Most of the time – they get it right!

SBA loans are offered by the Federal government to help small businesses grow that already have great potential. Most business owners go through training and a certification program to determine eligibility.

Go Fund Me Accounts are great ways to raise money very fast. Hundreds sometimes thousands of other people (strangers) though social media can examine and buy into your vision. They in turn can *gift-you* money to start your business. Donations can be as low as $10, and can be accomplished through the internet.

Peer to peer financing (P2P). You can learn more about this type of financing at www.prosper.com or www.lendingclub.com. These are other businesses just like yourself, but have been operating longer and are running successful. They in-turn pool their money to help other small start-up businesses.

Some business fail because they cannot fulfill or totally fulfill their obligations. That's why the previous session on **cash flow** is so important. Your Banker will want to see your **cash flow statement** and use that to decide whether not he/she will make you a loan. Please keep in mind that it is not his decision alone. If he feels good about your business, he will then take your file (your **financial statements** and **business plan**) to a **Committee**. The Committee consist of several people who work for the bank that participate in decision-making.

Buying an Existing Business

Your goals in buying an existing business should be the same as starting one from scratch:

1. Do I have the passion and commitment to stay and learn how to be a leader and business owner?
2. Do I have the money for startup, and training?
3. Is my product or service good enough to capture a significant market share?
4. Do I have a reasonable chance with hard work, tenacity and perseverance to succeed?
5. Do you have a knack for sales? Do you enjoy working with the public?
6. Are you comfortable making cold-calls to pitch your service or product?

Take yourself through a mini-evaluation. Assess your skills, work experience and interest. Jot them down here before contemplating buying an existing business:

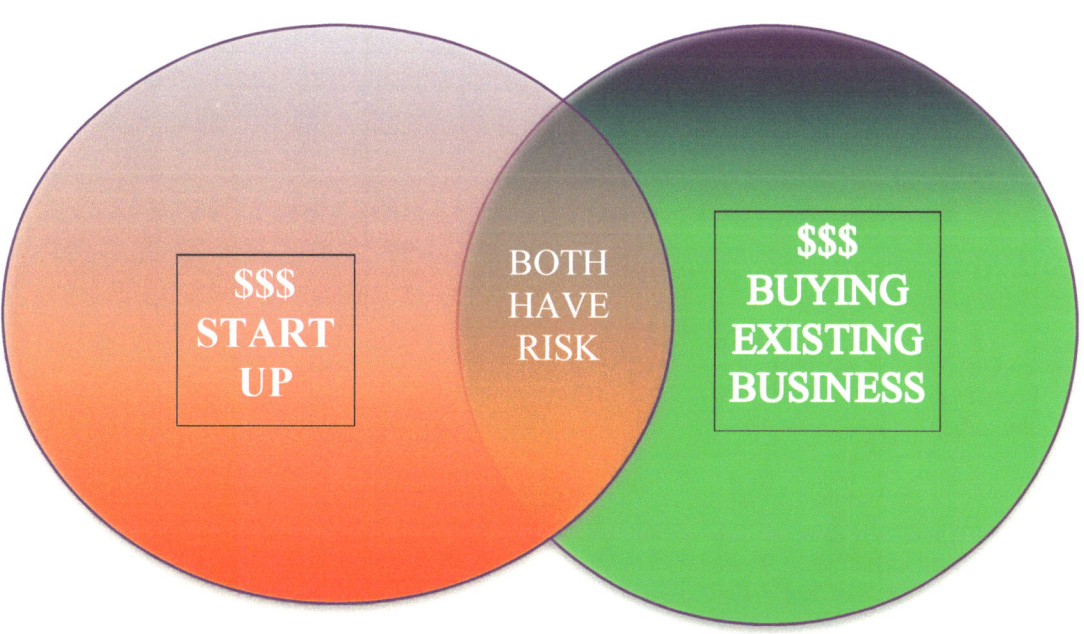

Evaluating the purchase of an existing business

Use this think-sheet as a scratch pad for evaluating the purchase of an existing business. Select 2 small businesses in your community that are for sale (want-ads) or that you would consider purchasing:

	#1	#2
Business name		
Product of service		
Cash to purchase		
Are you a sole Proprietor, Partnership or Corporation?		
Existing years in business		
Location (address)		
Am I buying this business to provide a job for myself, or will this be a long-tem investment? Did I thoroughly do my homework? Do I believe and will use the product or service that I'm thinking about buying? What do you know about the industry? Have to talked or visited other owners and their businesses? How many competing businesses in the same neighborhood? Are these competing businesses well established?		

Do they offer the same product or services at a lower or higher price? Does the product or service generate repeat demand? Is the demand for the product or service seasonal? Is the business currently widely recognizable? Are there any monthly re-occurring or franchise fees? Is financing available?		
How are decisions made? Who is the parent company? How much input do I have on day- to- day- operations? Does the company already have a reputation for quality products or services? Will the existing owner stay on for a period of time to train and guide me after the purchase? Will the owner stay on for a period of time to lend supervision and management help? Are their any contracts for suppliers that will be be passed on (ex: relationships with other vendors)?		

Page 2

Decision Grid

Now you have a blank slate: Fill in the pro's and cons of you starting up a business from scratch or buying an existing business?

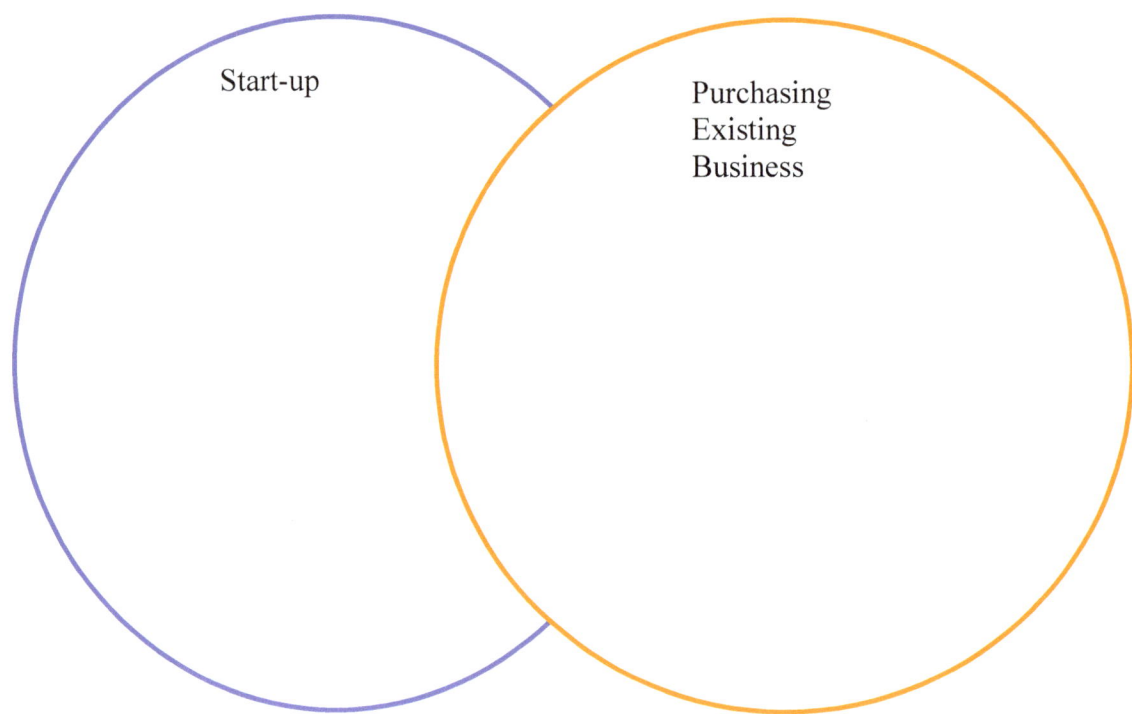

	Pros	Cons

Kidpreneur Forrest Mars Sr.

(March 21, 1904 – July 1, 1999) was an American businessman and the driving force of the **Mars** candy empire. He is best known for introducing the **Milky Way Bar** in 1923, the Mars Chocolate Candy Bars, **M&M's** in 1941, and Uncle Ben's Rice. He was the son of candy company founder Frank C. Mars and Ethel G. Mars.

Mars was born in Wadena, Minnesota, and raised in Saskatchewan, Canada after his parents' divorce. He rarely saw his father. After high school he entered the University of California, Berkeley and later transferred to Yale University, where he completed a degree in industrial engineering in 1928.

As an adult, Forrest Mars reunited with his father at Mars; however, the pair ran into a disagreement when Forrest wanted to expand abroad while his father did not. Mars then took a buyout from his father and moved to England where he created the Mars bar. In Europe, Mars briefly worked for Nestlé and the Tobler Company.

After he returned to the United States, Mars started his own food business- Food Products Manufacturing, where he established the Uncle Ben's Rice line and a pet food business, **Pedigree**. In partnership later with Bruce Murrie, Mars developed M&M's, the chocolate candy covered in a crunchy shell which "melts in your mouth, not in your hands," in 1940. They were modeled after a candy that he had discovered while in Spain during the 1930s. It is believed that he got the idea when he saw soldiers eating a similar candy during the Spanish Civil War. **Peanut M&M's** were introduced in 1954 although Forrest had been allergic to peanuts his entire life.

Following the death of his father, Forrest Mars took over the family business, Mars, Inc, merging it with his own company in 1964. Mars retired from Mars, Inc. in 1973, turning the company over to his children; Forrest Jr, John, and Jacqueline.

In 1980, retired and living in Henderson, Nevada, he founded Ethel M Chocolates, named after his mother. Ethel M was purchased by Mars, Inc. in 1988. Mars died at age 95 in Miami, Florida, having amassed a fortune of $4 billion. He was ranked as 30th in *Forbes* magazine's list of richest Americans (Forrest Jr. and John were 29th and 31st, respectively). He left the business jointly to his three children. Mars was inducted into the Junior Achievement U.S. Business Hall of Fame in 1984.

Sources: http://web.mit.edu/invent/iow/mars.html; Allen, Lawrence (2010). ChocolateFortunes.

Discussion questions

1. Who was Forrest Mars Sr.? Use the internet and research all the products he invented:

2. Why was he successful?

3. Who owns the business now?

4. How has the business changed?

5. Has the company been involved in any mergers or acquisitions?

6. How has Forrest Mars inspired you to be a Kidpreneur?

Kidpreneur Milton Snavely Hershey

Born: September 13, 1857 at Derry Township, Pennsylvania
Died: October 13, 1945 at Hershey, Pennsylvania
Best known for: Founding the Hershey Chocolate Corporation

Milton Snavely Hershey was born on September 13, 1857 in the small town of Derry, Pennsylvania. He only had one sibling, a sister named Serina who sadly died from Scarlet fever when Milton was nine years old. His father, Henry, was a dreamer who was constantly starting new jobs and working on his next *get rich quick* scheme. Like many young people of the time, Milton was expected to help out on the family farm. He learned early on of the value of hard work and perseverance. Henry Hershey, his father, rarely stayed anywhere very long, and was prone to leaving his wife and child for long periods. Because of this, Hershey had a very limited education with no schooling after 4th grade. He had two and a half years of education.

After the fourth grade (1871), his mother decided that Milton should leave school and learn a trade. Milton's mom found him a job as an apprentice to a printer. One day at work there, he accidentally dropped his hat in one of the machines. Because his boss was hot-tempered, he was fired shortly after. He thought the work was boring and didn't enjoy the job anyway. Though his father asked the printer to give him his job back, his mother arranged for the now 14-year-old Hershey to be apprenticed to a Lancaster County (1872) confectioner named Joseph Royer. Over the next four years, Hershey learned the craft of creating confections. In 1876, he moved to Philadelphia to start his first confectionery business.

At age 19 he had opened his second business, and had learned how to make caramels using fresh milk and all sorts of candy including peppermints, and fudge. He then went to New Orleans and Chicago looking for opportunities, before settling in New York City in 1883. He really enjoyed being a candy maker and thought he knew what he wanted to do for the rest of his life; but, no matter how hard Milton worked, he couldn't figure out how to get his business to make a profit. He worked harder and harder, but soon he ran out of money and had to shut his business down. Milton wasn't one to give up. His third shop failed, too. He just could not make enough money to keep it open.

He moved back home to Lancaster in 1900. Once again Milton started a new candy business. This time he would specialize in making just caramels. His caramel company was a huge success employing over 1,300 workers in two factories. After a travel to Chicago for the

World's Columbian Exposition, he took an interest in chocolate. After a long time of deciding, he took a risk and sold Lancaster Caramel Company for one million dollars to start the famous **Hershey Chocolate Company.**

Using the proceeds from the 1900 sale of the Lancaster Caramel Company, Hershey initially acquired farm land roughly 30 miles northwest of Lancaster. People thought he was crazy, because the land was surrounded by dairy farms. There, he could obtain the large supplies of fresh milk needed to perfect and produce fine milk chocolate.

Before long, Milton had to open up new candy making factories and branches all over the country. He sold his caramel business for $1 million and put all his efforts into making chocolate. He wanted to make a huge chocolate factory where he could mass produce chocolate so it would be both delicious and affordable for the average person. People thought he was crazy! Milton, however, didn't care. He went ahead with his plan and built the town of Hershey, Pennsylvania. It had lots of houses, a post office, churches, and schools. The chocolate company was a huge success. Soon Hershey's chocolates were the most famous chocolates in the world. On March 2, 1903, he began construction on what was to become the world's largest chocolate manufacturing company. The facility, completed in 1905, was designed to manufacture chocolate using the latest mass production techniques. Hershey was excited by the potential of milk chocolate, which at that time was a luxury product. Hershey was determined to develop a formula for milk chocolate and sell it to the American public. Through trial and error, he created his own formula for milk chocolate. Hershey's milk chocolate quickly became the first nationally marketed product of its kind.

The first Hershey bar was produced in 1900. **Hershey's Kisses** were developed in 1907, and the **Hershey's Bar with almonds** was introduced in 1908.

Why was Hershey successful?
Milton Hershey was more than just a candy maker and a dreamer, he was a good businessman and learned from his earlier mistakes. He was persistent, and would not give up. When he first started making chocolate, he made one simple product: the milk chocolate candy bar. Because he made so many, he could sell them at a low price. This allowed everyone to afford chocolate. Milton also hired good people, advertised his chocolates, and invested in other aspects of chocolate making like the production of sugar. He and his wife Kitty were not able to have children. He used his millions to invest in a school for orphaned boys called the Hershey Industrial School. He died at the age of 88 on October 13, 1945.

Discussion Questions

1. Who was Milton Hershey? Use the internet and research all the products he invented:

2. Why was he successful?

3. Who owns the business now?

4. How has the business changed?

5. Has the company been involved in any mergers or acquisitions?

6. What was the biggest lesson you learned from Milton Hershey?

Taxes & Insurance

I think it's very important that we close out this book with talking about taxes. There are costs in this world to do everything. Schools, parks, our armed forces, fire fighters, police, and libraries all function because of taxes.

Although there are many types of taxes, for the purposes of Kidpreneur 101, we will discuss **sales taxes**. Sales taxes are the most common, second to property tax and income taxes. The tax on sales made within a single state is almost always calculated based on the seller's location.

Sales taxes are extra charges a customer pays on items he or she purchases for his/her own use at the time he makes the purchase. When a customer makes a purchase, he pays the tax and his responsibility pretty much ends there. This is where the Kidpreneur's responsibility begins. You collect the tax and then send it to the appropriate taxing authority along with a tax return that explains how you arrived at the amount you're remitting. This is usually done on a quarterly basis.

Insurance

The purpose of insurance to transfer some of the **risk** that you could not afford to pay on your own. Your investors will want to know that you have this coverage or protection; moreover, some types of insurance will more than likely be required by your landlord. There are many types of insurance. As a Kidpreneur, you will probably only deal with two: **business property** and **liability insurance**.

Business property insurance will cover your supplies, your computers, and the equipment that you use in your company. It will also cover your loss of income from theft, floods, fires, hurricanes, earthquakes and other man-made disasters.

Liability insurance provides coverage to third parties, or if someone falls in your place of business and gets hurt. This insurance also protects you if you harm someone unintentionally with your product or service.

Final Thoughts

You **MUST** set aside time to work on your **business plan** and revise it as your business grows.

Be optimistic about your **long and short term goals.**

Change is good. Write your initial business plan in pencil. You can commit it to ink later.

Become REALLY good with accounting. Take a class. Learn how to count your own money, and project your own **profits**.

Never be satisfied! Focus and refine your product or service. Expansion should always be a goal for the future.

Remember as you revise your business plan, always use the **what- where- why and-how approach.**

Use the templates. Make copies when you feel comfortable with your business plan. You can add charts and graphs. Don't forget to start working on a logo for your business.

Have your business plan critiqued by persons already running successful companies.

Test and refine your business model often.

Share your business plan with your parents, your friends, or your trusted advisors.

Be sure you have current market data before you start. You will need to know the demographics of the neighborhood to which you are marketing your service or selling your product.

Very important - plan for catastrophic events! Back up your data, secure business and personal property insurance.

Protect your credit.

Be **REALLY** realistic!

Reading List

Teen Business Blast Off- Learn what makes a good idea great, who can help, and what skills you need as you follow ten teens who put their ideas to the test!

The Student Success Manifesto: Having trouble deciding what you're going to do after you graduate from school? Do you simply want to take your life to the next level? "The Student Success Manifesto" will help you leverage the entrepreneurial mindset to define and achieve success regardless of your career path.

Upstarts- Generation Y is creating startups at an unprecedented rate, and their approach to business is unlike anything you've seen. The generation described by the media as spoiled, entitled, even narcissistic, is proving these notions false every day. Inspired by the rock-star entrepreneurs of previous generations and driven by a burning desire to control their own destinies, GenY is rewriting the entrepreneurial playbook one cool startup at a time.

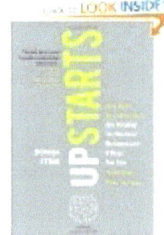

Filled with delightfully simple business ideas, *Better than a Lemonade Stand!* is a fun guide packed with creative ideas that show how to start a business with little or no start-up costs, attract and retain customers, develop negotiating skills, and more.
Originally written and published when the author was only fifteen years old, *Better than a Lemonade Stand!* has already helped thousands of kids start their own profitable small businesses. Now an adult and father himself, Daryl Bernstein has polished and expanded his book for a new generation of budding entrepreneurs.

Get ready to meet some amazing entrepreneurial superstars who are living their dreams and making a big difference doing it. They've shared their stories to inspire you, teach you, and show you that your own opportunities are endless. How did they discover their passion? What were their first steps to building their business? Who supported them along the way? Why do they all choose to give back to their community? In this book you'll learn the key principles that catapulted each of these incredible young entrepreneurs to success and how these same principles will lead you to a life of ultimate fulfillment.

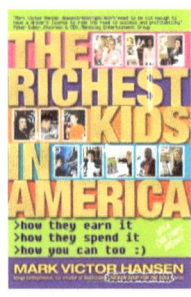

Appendix

Answers to *Do you know these financial terms?* pg. 21

1. savings account	9. safety deposit box	17. overdrawn	25. credit card
2. currency	10. withdraw	18. mortgage	26. NSF(non sufficient)
3. APR	11. deposit	19. promissory note	27. dime
4. endorsement	12. interest	20. coins	28. bankrupt
5. bank accounts	13. quarter	21. penny	29. endorse
6. CD	14. credit limit	22. statement	30. checking account
7. ATM	15. checkbook	23. vault	
8. $1.00/ a dollar	16. ink/pen	24. nickel	

Answers to *Word Scrabble* pg. 24

1. government	6. money	11. Franklin
2. seal	7. denomination	12. Treasury
3. Alibaba	8. counterfeit	13. notes
4. moolah	9. currency	14. deposit
5. Bureau	10. greenback	

Projecting profits – pg. 70.

Did Lisa consider that buying a used car may present its own share of problems? She will need to have money for unexpected repairs.

What if the car breaks down? She would have to borrow a car or use her parents charge card to Rent-A-Car to make deliveries.

What about car insurance? Since she's using it for a business, the insurance will be higher and she still only 18 years old.

Does Lisa have a contract with the drugstore or the office building? What if they decide to discontinue her services? That would devastate her business. That is a serious loss of income and now she's bought a car!

Build your own glossary

Angel investor

Asset

Balance sheet

Benchmarks

Board of directors

Business plan

Capital gains

Cash flow Statement

Collateral

Corporation

Decision grid

Depreciation

Dividend

Entrepreneur-
- One who sees an opportunity
- Makes a plan
- Starts the business and manages the business, and
- Receives the profit

Escrow

Fixed Cost

Insurance

Kidpreneur

Kidnovation

Kidpreneurship

Major investor

Merger

Net income

Operating budget

Partnership agreement

Peer-to Peer Lending

Promissory note

Profit

Raising Capital

Risk

Seed money

Secured loan

Taxes

Total Cost

Total Revenue

Unsecured loan

Variable Cost

Venture capitalist

Grateful to my Glory editor, thank you for having my back.

Dedicated to the little ones who make me smile
Ky, Karli & Ayden
Kayla & Casey
Caleb, Yael & Yosef
Myles, Lexie' & Mason
Ahymad, Mari' & Maurice
Marlon, Marcus & Vonnie'

Printed in the USA
CPSIA information can be obtained
at www.ICGtesting.com
LVHW061107070724
784836LV00002B/6